The Living
Flame of Love

The Living Flame of Love

JOHN OF THE CROSS

Translated by **DAVID LEWIS**

With an Introduction by
BARONESS CAROLINE COX

First published in Great Britain in 1919

This edition first published in Great Britain in 2017

Society for Promoting Christian Knowledge
36 Causton Street
London SW1P 4ST
www.spck.org.uk

British Library Cataloguing-in-Publication Data
A catalogue record for this book is available from the British Library

ISBN 978–0–281–07711–3
eBook ISBN 978–0–281–07712–0

Typeset by Graphicraft Limited, Hong Kong
First printed in Great Britain by Ashford Colour Press
Subsequently digitally printed in Great Britain

eBook by Graphicraft Limited, Hong Kong

Produced on paper from sustainable forests

Contents

Introduction

Caroline Cox

The works of John of the Cross (1542–91) are justly celebrated as milestones in Spanish literature as well as spiritual classics. Down the ages and still today, many people have found his poems and his prose commentaries valuable spiritual resources. In this brief introduction I want to highlight just some of the powerful imagery John uses in *The Living Flame*, and indicate how his work has spoken to me in ways relevant for my own life.

The powerful first impressions are an almost overwhelming 'sensual spirituality' combining passionate love of God with challenging images of pain, wounds and death. For example, using the image of fire, St John speaks of a log of wood which catches fire and becomes transformed into a greater fire, glowing more and more the longer it burns.

> So too the soul – and this is the subject of these stanzas – when transformed, and glowing interiorly in the fire of love, is not only united with the divine fire, but becomes a living flame, and itself conscious of it. The soul speaks of this with an intimate delicious sweetness of love, burning in its own flame, dwelling upon the various marvellous effects wrought within it.
>
> (Prologue 4)

This is an example of John's commitment to the celebration of the transcendent, without seeking to domesticate it.

Another image refers to 'rivers of living waters' (1.1), a reference to St John's Gospel (John 7.38). Use of images of nature to describe spiritual phenomena is, for me, one of the most inspirational characteristics of John's writing, which lifts his poetry on to a sublime plane. I also find the constant reference to Scripture spiritually helpful, grounding his work deeply in the Christian tradition.

Of course, the principal image in *The Living Flame* is that of the flame 'that woundest tenderly':

> Thus in this flame, the soul has so vivid a sense of God and a perception of him so sweet and delicious, that it cries out: 'O living flame of love!'
>
> That is, thou touchest me tenderly in thy love. For when this flame of divine life wounds the soul with the gentle languishing for the life of God, it wounds it with so much endearing tenderness, and softens it so that it melts away in love. The words of the bride in the Canticle are now fulfilled in the soul. 'My soul melted when he spoke' (Song of Songs 5.6). This is the effect in the soul when God speaks.   (1.7–8)

This is a wounding which heals the soul by causing it 'to melt away in love'. However, there is also the challenging recognition that fire can be painful and consuming: John highlights the theme of suffering with God, showing us our faults and giving us an awareness of sin. Again, John is so steeped in Scripture that he turns instinctively to Lamentations 3.1–7: 'He hath set me in dark places, as those that are dead for ever.' As in the famous Prologue to St John's Gospel (John 1.5), where the natural darkness inside us does not understand the supernatural light that invades it, John of the Cross explains to Christians who live in zones of 'comfortable Christianity' that taking up your cross and dying to yourself can lead to transformation in this flame that is the love of God (2.33). It is one of John's many gifts to us that he makes the self-sacrifice inherent in the Christian's spiritual life appealing.

It is not possible to venture very far into John's writing without uncovering allusions – sometimes quite shocking to us who live in Western culture – to images in the Song of Songs, in ways reminiscent of Bernard of Clairvaux before him. *The Living Flame* is no exception. He quotes Song of Songs 7.2: 'Thy belly as a heap of wheat compassed about with lilies' (3.8). John explains this by saying that the lilies are virtues that surround the bread of life (presumably an allusion to the Eucharist) and infuse in a person the knowledge of God. The person becomes 'a well of living waters which run with a strong stream from Mount Libanus' (3.8), where the mountain is God. This is another example of John's method of unpacking scriptural imagery and applying it to the soul in a way that echoes his deeply contemplative vision of human striving towards God and discloses the layers of that vision, revealing their relevance for every age.

The various images coalesce, revealing their flexibility. The Spirit can be both 'living flames of fire' and 'sweet water' (3.10). Referring to 'the deep caverns of sense' in Stanza 3, John explains that the 'caverns' are the powers of the soul: memory, understanding and will. Only the infinite can fill them, and, for this to happen, they need to be emptied and cleansed. But they tend to become filled with trifles and unable to recognize the infinite good or their own capacity for it (3.20). With this image, John puts into place a spirituality compatible with human psychology – it is perhaps no accident that both John and St Teresa of Avila are seen as anticipating many of Jung's insights into the depths of the mind.

Another evocative image is that of God as the Bridegroom and the soul as his spouse, echoing recurring themes from the Song of Songs. This gives rise to a whole series of fruitful meditations on the union and self-surrender of marriage, as well as the process of betrothal, which John sees as characterized by the giving of presents. He relates this idea of gift-giving to the state of spiritual betrothal, which he sees as God's way of preparing the soul for greater things (3.25–26).

I also find helpful John's explanation of the stages of the spiritual life. His exposition has a practical application: his description of the need in contemplative prayer to keep one's attention simply and lovingly on God echoes that of many other spiritual masters (3.36). John is also comfortingly reassuring and realistic, despite his often-proclaimed emphasis on the absolute. For example, he says that if you are not going backwards you are going forwards towards God! And, while he highlights the challenge of the spiritual ideal of perfect detachment in order to love God more than anything (3.55), he is helpfully (for me) realistic in setting out the obstacles that people can create for themselves in seeking God (3.76). This balance between the ideal and the realistic, with the recognition of the great gap between the goal of ultimate perfection and the harsh reality of our humanity, are features of John's writing that I find deeply reassuring. They help me to see that the sometimes ethereal and abstruse images in John's teaching are relevant to modern life. This encourages me to work harder to uncover the riches which abound in the depths of his evocative and often complex writing – and I hope you will be encouraged and blessed in the same way.

I end with his concluding words as they epitomize the essential spirit of faith, hope and love which inspires and infuses his work – and as he himself says, 'This is the reason why I say nothing more.'

> I would not speak of this breathing of God, neither do I wish to do so, because I am certain that I cannot; and indeed were I to speak of it, it would seem then to be something less than what it is in reality. This breathing of God is in the soul, in which in the awakening of the deep knowledge of the Divinity, He breathes the Holy Ghost according to the measure of that knowledge which absorbs it most profoundly, which inspires it most tenderly with love according to what it saw. This breathing is full of grace and glory, and therefore the Holy Ghost fills the soul with goodness and glory, whereby he inspires it with the love of himself, transcending all glory and all understanding. This is the reason why I say nothing more.   (4.19)

The Living
Flame of Love

Prologue

It is not without some unwillingness that, at the requests of others, I enter upon the explanation of the four stanzas because they relate to matters so interior and spiritual as to baffle the powers of language. The spiritual transcends the sensual, and he speaks but indifferently of the mind of the spirit who has not a spiritual mind himself. I have, therefore, in consideration of my own defects, put off this matter until now. But now that our Lord seems in some way to have opened to me the way of knowledge herein, and to have given me some fervour of spirit, I have resolved to enter on the subject. I know too well that of myself I can say nothing to the purpose on any subject; how much less then on a matter of such depth and substance as this! What is mine here will be nothing but defects and errors, and I therefore submit the whole to the better judgement and discretion of our Holy Mother the Catholic Roman Church, under whose guidance no one goeth astray. And now having said this, I will venture, in reliance on the Holy Writings, to give utterance to what I may have learned, observing at the same time that all I say falls far short of that which passes in this intimate union of the soul with God.

2. There is nothing strange in the fact that God bestows favours so great and so wonderful upon those souls whom he is pleased to comfort. For if we consider that it is God himself as God, and with infinite love and goodness, who bestows them, and this being

the case, they will not seem unreasonable, for he hath said himself that the Father and the Son and the Holy Ghost will come to him that loves him, and will dwell in him (John 14.23). And this is accomplished in making such an one live and abide in the Father, the Son and the Holy Ghost, in the life of God, as it shall be explained in the stanzas that follow.

3. In the former stanzas I spoke of the highest degree of perfection to which it is possible to attain in this life, transformation in God;[1] yet these, the explanation of which I now propose to undertake, speak of that love still more perfect and complete in the same state of transformation. For though it is true that the former and the present stanzas refer to one and the same state of transformation, and that no soul can pass beyond it as such, still with time and habits of devotion, the soul is more perfected and grounded in it. Thus, when a log of wood is set on fire, and when it is transformed into fire and united with it, the longer it burns and the hotter the fire, the more it glows until sparks and flames are emitted from it.

4. So too the soul – and this is the subject of these stanzas – when transformed, and glowing interiorly in the fire of love, is not only united with the divine fire, but becomes a living flame, and itself conscious of it. The soul speaks of this with an intimate delicious sweetness of love, burning in its own flame, dwelling upon the various marvellous effects wrought within it. These effects I now proceed to describe, following the same method: that is, I shall first transcribe the four stanzas, then each separately, and finally each line by itself as I explain them.

Stanzas[2]

1

O living flame of love,
That woundest tenderly my soul in its inmost depth!
As thou art no longer grievous,
Perfect thy work, if it be thy will,
Break the web of this sweet encounter.

2

O sweet burn!
O delicious wound!
O tender hand! O gentle touch!
Savouring of everlasting life,
And paying the whole debt,
By slaying thou hast changed death into life.

3

O lamps of fire,
In the splendours of which
The deep caverns of sense,
Dim and dark,
With unwonted brightness
Give light and warmth together to the Beloved.

4

How gently and how lovingly
Thou awakest in my bosom.
Where thou secretly dwellest alone;
And in thy sweet breathing,
Full of grace and glory,
How tenderly thou fillest me with thy love.

Stanza 1

O living flame of love,
That woundest tenderly my soul in its inmost depth!
As thou art no longer grievous,
Perfect thy work, if it be thy will,
Break the web of this sweet encounter.

Explanation

The bride of Christ, now feeling herself to be all on fire in the divine union, and that rivers of living waters are flowing from her belly, as Christ our Lord said (John 7.38) they would flow from the like souls, believes that, as she is transformed in God with such vehemence and so intimately possessed by him, so richly adorned with gifts and graces, she is near unto bliss, and that a slender veil only separates her from it. Seeing, too, that this sweet flame of love burning within her, each time it touches her makes her as it were glorious with foretaste of glory, so much so that whenever it absorbs and assails her, it seems to be admitting her to everlasting life, and to rend the veil of her mortality, she addresses herself, with a great longing, to the flame, which is the Holy Ghost, and prays him to destroy her mortal life in this sweet encounter, and bestow upon her in reality what he seems about to give, namely, perfect glory, crying: 'O living flame of love!'

'O living flame of love'

2. In order to express the fervour and reverence with which the soul is speaking in these four stanzas, it begins them with 'O' and 'How', which are significant of great earnestness, and whenever uttered show that something passes within that is deeper than the tongue can tell. 'O' is the cry of strong desire, and of earnest supplication, in the way of persuasion. The soul employs it in both senses here, for it magnifies and intimates its great desire, calling upon love to end its mortal life.

3. This flame of love is the Spirit of the Bridegroom, the Holy Ghost, of whose presence within itself the soul is conscious not only as fire which consumes it, and transforms it in sweet love, but as a fire burning within it, sending forth a flame which bathes it in glory and recreates it with the refreshment of everlasting life. The work of the Holy Ghost in a soul transformed in his love is this: his interior action within it is to kindle it and set it on fire; this is the burning of love, in union with which the will loves most deeply, being now one by love with that flame of fire. And thus the soul's acts of love are most precious, and even one of them more meritorious than many elicited not in the state of transformation. The transformation in love differs from the flame of love as a habit differs from an act, or as the glowing fuel from the flames it emits, the flames being the effect of the fire which is there burning.

4. Hence then we may say of the soul which is transformed in love, that its ordinary state is that of the fuel in the midst of the fire; that the acts of such a soul are the flames which rise up out of the fire of love, vehement in proportion to the intensity of the fire of union, and to the rapture and absorption of the will in the flame of the Holy Ghost; rising like the angel who ascended to God in the flame

which consumed the holocaust of Manoah (Judg. 13.20). And as the soul, in its present condition, cannot elicit these acts without a special inspiration of the Holy Ghost, all these acts must be divine, in so far as the soul is under the special influence of God. Hence then it seems to the soul, as often as the flame breaks forth, causing it to love sweetly with a heavenly disposition, that its life everlasting is begun, and that its acts are divine in God.

5. This is the language in which God addresses purified and stainless souls, namely, words of fire. 'Thy word', saith the Psalmist, 'is a vehement fire' (Ps. 119.140). And in Jeremiah we read, 'are not my words as a fire? saith our Lord' (Jer. 23.29). His 'words', we learn from himself, 'are spirit and life' (John 6.63); the power and efficacy of which are felt by such souls as have ears to hear; pure souls full of love. But those souls whose palate is not healthy, whose desire is after other things, cannot perceive the spirit and life of his words. And therefore the more wonderful the words of the Son of God, the more insipid they are to some who hear them, because of the impurity in which they live.

6. Thus, when he announced the doctrine of the Holy Eucharist, a doctrine full of sweetness and of love, 'many of his disciples went back' (John 6.67). If such persons as these have no taste for the words of God which he speaks inwardly to them, it is not to be supposed that all others are like them. St Peter loved the words of Christ, for he replied, 'Lord, to whom shall we go? Thou hast the words of eternal life' (John 6.68). The woman of Samaria forgot the water, and 'left her water pot' (John 4.28) at the well, because of the sweetness of the words of God.

7. And now when the soul has drawn so near unto God as to be transformed in the flame of love, when the Father and the Son and the Holy Ghost are in communion with it, is it anything incredible

to say that it has a foretaste – though not perfectly, because this life admits not of it – of everlasting life in this fire of the Holy Ghost? This is the reason why this flame is said to be a living flame, not because it is not always living, but because its effect is to make the soul live spiritually in God, and to be conscious of such a life, as it is written, 'My heart and my flesh have rejoiced toward the living God' (Ps. 84.2). The Psalmist makes use of the word 'living' not because it was necessary, for God is ever-living, but to show that the body and the spirit had a lively feeling of God; that is the rejoicing in the living God. Thus in this flame, the soul has so vivid a sense of God and a perception of him so sweet and delicious, that it cries out: 'O living flame of love!'

'That woundest tenderly'

8. That is, thou touchest me tenderly in thy love. For when this flame of divine life wounds the soul with the gentle languishing for the life of God, it wounds it with so much endearing tenderness, and softens it so that it melts away in love. The words of the bride in the Canticle are now fulfilled in the soul. 'My soul melted when he spoke' (Song of Songs 5.6). This is the effect in the soul when God speaks.

9. But how can we say that it wounds the soul, when there is nothing to wound, seeing that it is all consumed in the fire of love? It is certainly marvellous; for as fire is never idle, but in continual movement, flashing in one direction, then in another, so love, the function of which is to wound, so as to cause love and joy, when it exists in the soul as a living flame, darts forth its most tender flames of love, causing wounds, exerting joyously all the arts and wiles of love as in the palace of its wedding feast. So Assuerus exhibited his riches, and the glory of his power at 'the wedding and marriage of Esther' (Esth. 2.18); and so is wrought in the soul what is read in the Proverbs:

I 'was delighted every day . . . playing in the world, and my delights were to be with the children of men' (Prov. 8.30, 31, that is, to give myself to them. This wounding, therefore, which is the 'playing' of divine wisdom, is the flames of those tender touches which touch the soul continually, touches of the fire of love which is never idle. And of these flashings of the fire it is said that they wound the soul in its inmost substance.

'My soul in its inmost depth'

10. The feast of the Holy Ghost is celebrated in the substance of the soul, which is inaccessible to the devil, the world, and the flesh; and therefore the more interior the feast, the more secure, substantial and delicious it is. For the more interior it is, the purer it is; and the greater the purity, the greater the abundance, frequency and universality of God's communication of himself; and thus the joy of the soul and spirit is so much the greater, for it is God himself who is the author of all this, and the soul doeth nothing of itself, in the sense I shall immediately explain.

11. And inasmuch as the soul cannot work naturally here, nor make any efforts of its own otherwise than through the bodily senses and by their help – of which it is in this case completely free, and from which it is most detached – the work of the soul is solely to receive what God communicates, who alone in the depths of the soul, without the help of the senses, can influence and direct it, and operate within it. Thus, then, all the movements of such a soul are divine, and though of God, still they are the soul's, because God effects them within it, itself willing them and assenting to them.

12. The expression, 'inmost depth' implies other depths of the soul less profound, and it is necessary to consider this. In the first place the soul, regarded as spirit, has neither height nor depth of greater

or less degree in its own nature, as bodies have which have bulk. The soul has no parts, neither is there any difference between its interior and exterior, for it is uniform; it has no depths of greater or less profundity, nor can one part of it be more enlightened than another, as is the case with physical bodies, for the whole of it is enlightened uniformly at once.

13. Setting aside this signification of depth, material and measurable, we say that the inmost depth of the soul is there where its being, power and the force of its action and movement penetrate and cannot go further. Thus fire, or a stone, tend by their natural force to the centre of their sphere, and cannot go beyond it, or help resting there, unless some obstacle intervene. Accordingly, when a stone lies on the ground it is said to be within its centre, because within the sphere of its active motion, which is the element of earth, but not in the inmost depth of that centre, the middle of the earth, because it has still power and force to descend thither, provided all that hinders it be taken away. So when it shall have reached the centre of the earth, and is incapable of further motion of its own, we say of it that it is then in its inmost or deepest centre.

14. The centre of the soul is God. When the soul shall have reached him, according to its essence, and according to the power of its operations, it will then have attained to its ultimate and deepest centre in God. This will be when the soul shall love him, comprehend him and enjoy him with all its strength. When, however, the soul has not attained to this state, though it be in God, who is the centre of it by grace and communion with him, still if it can move further and is not satisfied, though in the centre, it is not in the deepest centre, because there is still room for it to advance.

15. Love unites the soul with God, and the greater its love the deeper does it enter into God, and the more is it centred in him.

According to this way of speaking, we may say that as the degrees of love, so are the centres which the soul finds in God. These are the many mansions of the Father's house (John 14.2). Thus, a soul which has but one degree of love is already in God, who is its centre: for one degree of love is sufficient for our abiding in him in the state of grace. If we have two degrees of love we shall then have found another centre, more interiorly in God; and if we have three we shall have reached another and more interior centre still.

16. But if the soul shall have attained to the highest degree of love, the love of God will then wound it in its inmost depth or centre and the soul will be transformed and enlightened in the highest degree in its substance, faculties and strength, until it shall become most like unto God. The soul in this state may be compared to crystal, lucid and pure; the greater the light thrown upon it, the more luminous it becomes by the concentration thereof, until at last it seems to be all light and undistinguishable from it; it being then so illumined, and to the utmost extent, that it seems to be one with the light itself.

17. The flame wounds the soul in its inmost depth; that is, it wounds it when it touches the very depths of its substance, power and force. This expression implies that abundance of joy and bliss, which is the greater and the more tender, the more vehemently and substantially the soul is transformed and centred in God. It greatly surpasses that which occurs in the ordinary union of love, for it is in proportion to the greater heat of the fire of love which now emits the living flame. The soul which has the fruition only of the ordinary union of love may be compared, in a certain sense, to the 'fire' of God which is in Sion, that is, in the Church militant; while the soul which has the fruition of glory so sweet may be compared to 'his furnace in Jerusalem' (Isa. 31.9), which means the vision of peace.

18. The soul in the burning furnace is in a more peaceful, glorious and tender union, the more the flame of the furnace transcends the fire of ordinary love. Thus the soul, feeling that the living flame ministers to it all good – divine love brings all blessings with it – cries out: 'O living flame of love, that woundest tenderly.' The cry of the soul is: O kindling burning love, how tenderly dost thou make me glorious by thy loving movements in my greatest power and strength, giving me a divine intelligence according to the capacity of my understanding, and communicating love according to the utmost freedom of my will; that is, thou hast elevated to the greatest height, by the divine intelligence, the powers of my understanding in the most intense fervour and substantial union of my will. This ineffable effect then takes place when this flame of fire rushes upwards in the soul. The divine wisdom absorbs the soul – which is now purified and most clean – profoundly and sublimely in itself; for 'wisdom reacheth everywhere by reason of her purity' (Wisd. 7.24). It is in this absorption of wisdom that the Holy Ghost effects those glorious quiverings of his flame of which I am speaking. And as the flame is so sweet, the soul says: 'As thou art no longer grievous.'

'As thou art no longer grievous'

19. Thou dost not afflict, nor vex, nor weary me as before. This flame, when the soul was in the state of spiritual purgation, that is, when it was entering that of contemplation, was not so friendly and sweet as it is now in the state of union. In order to explain this we must dwell a little on this point. For before the divine fire enters into the soul and unites itself to it in its inmost depth by the complete and perfect purgation and purity thereof, the flame, which is the Holy Ghost, wounds it, destroys and consumes the imperfections of its evil habits. This is the work of the Holy Ghost, who thereby

disposes the soul for its divine union and a substantial transformation in God by love. For the flame which afterwards unites itself to the soul, glorifying it, is the very same which before assailed and purified it; just as the fire which ultimately penetrates the substance of the fuel is the very same which in the beginning darted its flames around it, playing about it, and depriving it of its ugliness until it prepared it with its heat for its own entrance into it, and transformation of it into itself.

20. The soul suffers greatly in this spiritual exercise, and endures grievous afflictions of spirit which occasionally overflow into the senses; for then the flame is felt to be grievous, for in this state of purgation the flame does not burn brightly but is darksome, and if it gives forth any light at all it is only to show to the soul and make it feel all its miseries and defects; neither is it sweet but painful, and if it kindles a fire of love that fire causes torments and uneasiness; it does not bring delight but aridity, for although God in his kindness may send the soul some comfort to strengthen and animate it he makes it pay, both before and after, with sufferings and trials. It is not a refreshing and peaceful fire, but a consuming and searching one that makes the soul faint away and grieve at the sight of self; not a glorious brightness, for it embitters the soul and makes it miserable, owing to the spiritual light it throws on self, for, as Jeremiah says, God 'hath sent fire into my bones' (Lam. 1.13), or, in the words of David, 'Thou hast tried me by fire' (Ps. 17.3). Thus, at this juncture, the soul suffers in the understanding from deep darkness, in the will from aridity and conflict, and in the memory from the consciousness of its miseries – for the eye of the spiritual understanding is clear – and in its very substance the soul suffers from poverty and dereliction. Dry and cold, yea, at times, even hot, nothing gives it relief, nor has it a single good thought to console it and to help it to

lift up the heart to God, for this flame has made it 'grievous', even as Job said when he found himself in this plight: 'Thou art changed to be cruel toward me' (Job 30.21). Suffering all these things together the soul undergoes, as it were, its purgatory, for all happiness being taken away the torture is hardly inferior to the torments of purgatory.

I should scarcely know how to describe this 'grievousness', and what the soul feels and bears in it, were it not for these telling words of Jeremiah: 'I am the man that see my poverty by the rod of his indignation; he hath led me, and brought me into darkness and not into light. Only against me he hath turned, and turned again his hand all the day. My skin and my flesh he hath made old, he hath broken my bones. He hath built round about me, and he hath encompassed me with gall and labour. He hath set me in dark places, as those that are dead for ever. He hath built against me round about, that I may not get out: he hath made my fetters heavy' (Lam. 3.1–7). Jeremiah says a great deal more besides this in the same place; for this is the remedy and medicine chosen by God to restore health to the soul after its many infirmities, the cure being of a necessity commensurate to the disease. Here then, the heart is 'laid upon coals to drive away all kind of devils' (Tobit 6.8); here, too, all its maladies are brought to light, and openly exhibited before the eyes, and thus they are cured. Whatever may have been hidden within its depths now becomes visible and palpable to the soul by the glare and heat of that fire, for previously nothing could be seen. When the flame acts upon a log of wood steam and smoke are seen to issue in evidence of humidity and frigidity which were unsuspected beforehand. Thus the soul, near this flame, sees and feels clearly its miseries, because – O wonder! – there arise within it contraries at variance with each other, yet seated side by side, making war against each other on the battlefield of the soul, and striving, as the philosophers say, to expel each other so as to reign uppermost in the soul. The virtues and properties of God, being in the highest degree perfect, arise and make war within the soul, on the habits and properties of man which are in the highest degree imperfect. For since this flame gives forth a dazzling light it penetrates the darkness of the soul which, in its way, is profound in the extreme; the soul now feels its natural darkness oppose the supernatural light, without feeling the supernatural light itself, for 'the darkness does not comprehend it' (John 1.5). Rather, it feels its natural darkness only in so far as it is penetrated by light, for no soul can see its own darkness except by the side of the divine light until, the darkness being dissipated, itself becomes illumined and sees the light, the eye being now made clear and strong. For an intense light is to a weak sight, or an eye that is not wholly clear, nothing but darkness, because the excess of light destroys the power of seeing. For this reason the flame was 'grievous' to the eye of the understanding, for, being at once loving and tender, it lovingly and tenderly penetrates the will which, by its nature, is arid and hard. And as hardness is discovered when contrasted with tenderness, and aridity when compared with love, so the will comes to a knowledge of its own hardness and aridity when contrasted with God, though it does not feel the love and tenderness of the flame, for hardness and aridity cannot comprehend their contraries, until, being expelled by these, the love and tenderness of God reign supreme in the will, for two contraries cannot coexist in one subject. Similarly, the soul perceives its own smallness in comparison with the immensity of the flame, and suffers great uneasiness until the flame, acting on it, dilates it. Thus, the latter has proved 'grievous' to the will also, for the sweet nourishment of love is insipid to a palate not yet weaned from other affections. Finally, the soul, which of itself is exceedingly poor, having nothing whatever, nor the means of procuring any satisfaction, gains a knowledge of its poverty, misery and malice by contrasting them with the riches, goodness and delights possessed by this flame, for malice does not comprehend goodness, nor poverty riches, etc., until the flame succeeds in purifying the soul, and, while transforming it, enriches, glorifies and delights it too. In this manner the flame was at first 'grievous' to the soul, which suffers severely in its substance and powers from the uneasiness and anguish caused by the war of contraries within its ailing frame. Here, God who is all perfection, there the habits of imperfection of the soul; cauterizing it with a divine fire he extirpates them and leaves a well-prepared soil upon which he may enter with his gentle, peaceful and glorious love, as does a flame when it gets hold of wood.

So powerful a purgation is the lot of but few souls, namely of those whom he intends to lift by contemplation to some degree of union; the more sublime that degree, the fiercer the purification. When he resolves to snatch a soul from the common way of natural operations and to lead it to the spiritual life, from meditation to contemplation – which is heavenly rather than earthly life – and to communicate himself by the union of love, he begins by making himself known to the spirit, as yet impure and imperfect and full of evil habits. Each one suffers in proportion to his imperfections. This purgation is sometimes as fierce in its way as that of purgatory, for the one is meant to dispose the soul for a perfect union even here below, while the other is to enable it to see God hereafter. I shall say nothing here of the intention of this cleansing, the degrees of its intensity, its operation in the will, the understanding and the memory, in the substance of the soul, in all its powers, or in the sensitive part alone, nor how it may be ascertained whether it is this or that, at what time or at which precise point of the spiritual journey it begins, as all this has nothing to do with my present purpose; moreover, I have fully discussed it in my treatise on the Dark Night in the *Ascent of Mount Carmel*.[3] It is enough for us to know that God, who seeks to enter the soul by union and transformation of love, is he who previously assailed the soul, purifying it with the light and heat of his divine flame, just as it is the same fire that first disposes the wood for combustion and afterwards consumes it. Thus, the same which now is sweet, being seated within the soul, was at first 'grievous' while assailing it from without.

21. The meaning of the whole is as follows: thou art now not only not darkness as before, but the divine light of my understanding wherewith I behold thee: not only dost thou abstain from causing me to faint in my weakness, but thou art become the strength of my will, wherein I can love and enjoy thee, being wholly transformed by divine love. Thou art no longer grief and affliction, but rather my glory, my delight, and my liberty, seeing that the words of the Canticle may be said of me, 'Who is this that cometh up from the desert flowing with delights leaning upon her Beloved' (Song of Songs 8.5), scattering love on this side and on that? 'Perfect thy work, if it be thy will.'

'Perfect thy work, if it be thy will'

22. That is, do thou perfect the spiritual marriage in the beatific vision. Though it is true that the soul is the more resigned the more it is transformed, when it has attained to a state so high as this, for it knows nothing and seeks nothing with a view to itself (1 Cor. 13.5), but only in and for the Beloved – for Charity seeks nothing but the good and glory of the Beloved – still because it lives in hope, and hope implies a want, it groans deeply – though sweetly and joyfully – because it has not fully attained to the perfect adoption of the sons of God, in which, being perfected in glory, all its desires will

be satisfied. However intimate the soul's union may be with God, it will never be satisfied here below till his 'glory shall appear' (Ps. 17.15), especially because it has already tasted, by anticipation, of its sweetness.

23. That sweetness is such that if God had not had pity on its natural frailty and covered it with his right hand, as he did Moses, that he might not die when he saw the glory of God – for the natural powers of the soul receive comfort and delight from that right hand, rather than hurt – it would have died at each vibration of the flame, seeing that the inferior part thereof is incapable of enduring so great and so sharp a fire. This desire of the soul is therefore no longer painful, for its condition is now such that all pain is over, and its prayers are offered for the object it desires in great sweetness, joy and resignation. This is the reason why it says, 'if it be Thy will', for the will and desire are now so united in God, each in its own way, that the soul regards it as its glory that the will of God should be done in it. Such are now the glimpses of glory, and such the love which now shines forth, that it would argue but little love on its part if it did not pray to be admitted to the perfect consummation of love.

24. Moreover, the soul in the power of this sweet communication sees that the Holy Ghost incites it, and invites it in most wonderful ways, and by sweet affections, to this immeasurable glory, which he there sets before it, saying, 'Arise, make haste, my love, my dove, my beautiful one, and come. For winter is now past, the rain is gone and departed. The flowers have appeared in our land . . . The fig-tree hath brought forth her green figs, the flourishing vineyards have given their savour. Arise, my love, my beautiful one, and come; my dove in the holes of the rock, in the hollow places of the wall, show me thy face, let thy voice sound in mine ears, for thy voice is sweet,

and thy face comely' (Song of Songs 2.10–14). The soul hears all this spoken by the Holy Ghost in this sweet and tender flame, and therefore answers him, saying, 'Perfect thy work, if it be thy will,' thereby making the two petitions which our Lord commands, 'thy kingdom come, thy will be done' (Matt. 6.10), that is, give me thy kingdom according to thy will, and that it may be so 'Break the web of this sweet encounter.'

'Break the web of this sweet encounter'

25. That is, the hindrance to this so grand an affair. It is an easy thing to draw near unto God when all hindrances are set aside, and when the web that divides us from him is broken. There are three webs to be broken before we can have the perfect fruition of God:

1 The temporal web, which comprises all created things.
2 The natural web, which comprises all mere natural actions and inclinations.
3 The web of sense, which is merely the union of soul and body; that is, the sensitive and animal life, of which St Paul speaks, saying, 'For we know if our earthly house of this habitation be dissolved, that we have a building of God, a house not made with hands, eternal in heaven' (2 Cor. 5.1).

26. The first and second web must of necessity have been broken in order to enter into the fruition of God in the union of love, when we denied ourselves in worldly things and renounced them, when our affections and desires were mortified, and when all our operations became divine. These webs were broken in the assaults of this flame when it was still grievous. In the spiritual purgation the soul breaks the two webs I am speaking of, and becomes united with God; the third alone, the web of the life of sense, remains now to be

broken. This is the reason why but one web is mentioned here. For now one web alone remains, and this the flame assails not painfully and grievously as it assailed the others, but with great sweetness and delight.

27. Thus the death of such souls is most full of sweetness, beyond that of their whole spiritual life, for they die of the sweet violence of love, like the swan which sings more sweetly when death is nigh.

28. This is why the Psalmist said, 'Precious in the sight of our Lord is the death of his saints' (Ps. 116.15), for then the rivers of the soul's love flow into the sea of love, so wide and deep as to seem a sea themselves; the beginning and the end unite together to accompany the just departing for his kingdom. 'From the ends of the earth', in the words of Isaiah, are 'heard praises, the glory of the just one' (Isa. 24.16), and the soul feels itself in the midst of these glorious encounters on the point of departing in all abundance for the perfect fruition of the kingdom, for it beholds itself pure and rich, and prepared, so far as it is possible, consistently with the faith and the conditions of this life. God now permits it to behold its own beauty, and entrusts it with the gifts and graces he has endowed it with, for all this turns into love and praise without the stain of presumption or of vanity, because no leaven of imperfection remains to corrupt it.

29. When the soul sees that nothing is wanting but the breaking of the frail web of its natural life, by which its liberty is enthralled, it prays that it may be broken; for it longs 'to be dissolved and to be with Christ' (Phil. 1.23), to burst the bonds which bind the spirit and the flesh together, that both may resume their proper state, for they are by nature different, the flesh to 'return to its earth, and the spirit unto God who gave it' (Eccles. 12.7). The mortal body, as St John saith, 'profiteth nothing' (John 6.63), but is rather a hindrance to the good of the spirit. The soul, therefore, prays for the dissolution

of the body, for it is sad that a life so mean should be a hindrance in the way of a life so noble.

30. This life is called a web for three reasons:

1 Because of the connection between the spirit and the flesh.
2 Because it separates the soul and God.
3 Because a web is not so thick but that light penetrates it.

The connection between soul and body, in this state of perfection is so slight a web that the divinity shines through it, now that the soul is so spiritualized, made subtle and refined. When the power of the life to come is felt in the soul, the weakness of this life becomes manifest. Its present life seems to be but a slender web, even a spider's web, in the words of David, 'our years shall be considered as a spider' (Ps. 90.9), and even less than that, when the soul is raised to a state so high, for being raised so high, it perceives things as God does, in whose sight 'a thousand years are as yesterday which is past' (Ps. 90.4) and before whom 'all nations are as if they had no being at all' (Isa. 40.17). In the same way all things appear to the soul as nothing, yea, itself is nothing in its own eyes, and God alone is its all.

31. It may be asked here why the soul prays for the breaking of the web rather than for its cutting or its removal, since the effect would be the same in either case. There are four reasons which determine it.

The expression it employs is the most proper, because it is more natural that a thing should be broken in an encounter than that it should be cut or taken away.

Because love likes force, with violent and impetuous contacts, and these result in breaking rather than in cutting or taking away.

Because its love is so strong, it desires that the act of breaking the web may be done in a moment; the more rapid and spiritual the act, the greater its force and worth.

32. The power of love is now more concentrated and more vigorous, and the perfection of transforming love enters the soul, as form into matter, in an instant. Until now there was no act of perfect transformation, only the disposition towards it in desires and affections successively repeated, which in very few souls attain to the perfect act of transformation. Hence a soul that is disposed may elicit many more, and more intense acts in a brief period than another soul not so disposed in a long time, for this soul spends all its energies in the preparation of itself, and even afterwards the fire does not wholly penetrate the fuel it has to burn. But when the soul is already prepared, love enters in continuously, and the spark at the first contact seizes on the fuel that is dry. And thus the enamoured soul prefers the abrupt breaking of the web to its tedious cutting or waiting for its removal.

33. The fourth reason why the soul prays for the breaking of the web of life is its desire that it may be done quickly: for when we cut or remove anything we do it deliberately, when the matter is ripe, and then time and thought become necessary; but a violent rupture requires nothing of the kind. The soul's desire is not to wait for the natural termination of its mortal life, because the violence of its love and the disposition it is in incline it with resignation towards the violent rupture of its natural life in the supernatural assaults of love. Moreover, it knows well that it is the way of God to call such souls to himself before the time, that he fills them with good, and delivers them from evil, perfecting them in a short space, and bestowing upon them, through love, what they could have gained only by length of time. 'Pleasing God, he is made beloved, and living among sinners he was translated. He was taken away lest malice should change his understanding, or lest any guile deceive his soul. Being consummate in a short space, he fulfilled much time, for his soul pleased God; for

this cause he hastened to bring him out of the midst of iniquities'(Wisd. 4.10–14). The constant practice of love is therefore a matter of the last importance, for when the soul is perfect therein, its detention here below cannot be long before it is admitted to see God face to face.

34. But why is this interior assault of the Holy Ghost called an encounter? Though the soul is very desirous to see the end of its natural life, yet because the time is not yet come, that cannot be, and so God, to make it perfect and to raise it above the flesh more and more, assails it divinely and gloriously, and these assaults are really encounters wherein God penetrates the soul, deifies the very substance of it, and renders it as it were divine. The substance of God absorbs the soul, because he assails and pierces it to the quick by the Holy Ghost, whose communications are vehement when they are of fire as at present. The soul says this encounter is sweet, because it has therein a lively taste of God; not that many other touches and encounters of God, of which the soul is now the object, cease to be sweet and delicious, but on account of the pre-eminent sweetness of this; for God effects it in order to detach it perfectly and make it glorious. Hence the soul relying on his protection becomes bold, and says, 'Break the web of this sweet encounter.'

35. The whole stanza may be paraphrased as follows: O flame of the Holy Ghost, penetrating so profoundly and so tenderly the very substance of my soul, and burning it with thy heat, since thou art now so gentle as to manifest thy desire of giving thyself wholly to me in everlasting life; if formerly my petitions did not reach thine ears, when I was weary and worn with love, suffering through the weakness of sense and spirit, because of my great infirmities, impurity and little love, I prayed to be set free – for with desire hath my soul desired thee – when my impatient love would not suffer me to

submit to the conditions of this life according to thy will – for it was thy will that I should live – and when the previous impulses of my love were insufficient in thy sight, because there was no substance in them; now that I am grown strong in love, that body and soul together do not only follow after thee, but that my heart and my flesh rejoice in the living God (Ps. 84.2) with one consent, so that I am praying for that which thou willest I should pray for, and what thou willest not, that I pray not for – it seems even that I could not do it, neither does it enter into my mind to do so – and as my prayers are now more efficacious and more reasonable in thy sight, for they proceed from thee, and thou willest I should so pray, and as I pray in the joy and sweetness of the Holy Ghost, and 'my judgement cometh forth from thy countenance' (Ps. 17.2), when thou art pleased with my prayer and hearkenest to it – break thou the slender web of this life that I may be enabled to love thee hereafter with that fullness and abundance which my soul desires, without end for evermore.

Stanza 2

O sweet burn!
O delicious wound!
O tender hand! O gentle touch!
Savouring of everlasting life,
And paying the whole debt,
By slaying thou hast changed death into life.

Explanation

We learn here that it is the three Persons of the Most Holy Trinity, Father, Son and Holy Ghost, who accomplish the divine work of union in the soul. The 'hand', the 'touch' and the 'burn' are in substance one and the same; and the three terms are employed because they express effects peculiar to each. The 'burn' is the Holy Ghost; the 'hand ' is the Father; and the 'touch' is the Son. Thus the soul magnifies the Father, the Son and the Holy Ghost, extolling those three grand gifts and graces which they perfect within it, in that they have changed death into life, transforming it in themselves.

2. The first of these gifts is the delicious wound, attributed to the Holy Ghost, and so the soul calls it the 'burn'. The second is the 'taste of everlasting life', attributed to the Son, and the soul calls it the 'gentle touch'. The third is that 'gift' which is the perfect recompense of the soul, attributed to the Father, and is therefore called the 'tender hand'. Though the three Persons of the Most Holy Trinity are

referred to severally, because of the operations peculiar to each, the soul is addressing itself to but one essence, saying, 'Thou hast changed it into life', for the three divine Persons work together, and the whole is attributed to each, and to all.

'O sweet burn!'

3. In the book of Deuteronomy, Moses saith, 'Our Lord God is a consuming fire' (Deut. 4.24), that is, a fire of love. And as his power is infinite, he consumes infinitely, burning with great vehemence, and transforming into himself all he touches. But he burns everything according to the measure of its preparation, some more, others less; and also according to his own good pleasure, as and when and how he will. And as this is an infinite fire of love, so when he touches the soul somewhat sharply, the burning heat within it becomes so extreme as to surpass all the fires of the world. This is the reason why this touch of God is said to be a 'burn': for the fire there is more intense, and more concentrated, and the effect of it surpasses that of all other fires.

4. When the divine fire shall have transformed the soul into itself, the soul not only feels the burn, but itself is become wholly and entirely burnt up in this vehement fire. O how wonderful the fire of God! Though so vehement and so consuming, though it can destroy a thousand worlds with more ease than the material fire can destroy a single straw, it consumes not the spirit wherein it burns, but rather in proportion to its strength and heat, delights and deifies it, burning sweetly within according to the strength which God has given. Thus, on the day of Pentecost the fire descended with great vehemence upon the Apostles, who, according to St Gregory,[4] sweetly burned interiorly. The Church also says, when celebrating that event: 'The divine fire came down, not consuming but enlightening.'[5] For

as the object of these communications is to elevate the soul, the burning of the fire does not distress it but gladdens it, does not weary it but delights it, and renders it glorious and rich. This is the reason why it is said to be sweet.

5. Thus then the blessed soul, which by the mercy of God has been burnt, knoweth all things, tasteth all things, 'whatever it shall do shall prosper' (Ps. 1.3), against it nothing shall prevail, nothing shall touch it. It is of that soul that the Apostle said: 'The spiritual man judgeth all things, and he himself is judged of no man' (1 Cor. 2.15), for 'the Spirit searcheth all things, yea, the deep things of God' (1 Cor. 2.10), because it belongs to love to search into all that the Beloved has.

6. O, the great glory of the souls who are worthy of this supreme fire which, having infinite power to consume and annihilate you, consumes you not, but makes you infinitely perfect in glory! Wonder not that God should elevate some souls to so high a degree, for he alone is wonderful in his marvellous works. As this burn then is so sweet – as it is here said to be – how happy must that soul be which this fire has touched! The soul would speak of it, but cannot, so it says only, 'O delicious wound'.

'O delicious wound!'

7. He who inflicts the wound relieves and heals while he inflicts it. It bears some resemblance to the caustic usage of natural fire, which when applied to a wound increases it, and renders a wound, which iron or other instruments occasioned, a wound of fire. The longer the caustic is applied, the more grievous the wound, until the whole matter be destroyed. Thus the divine burn of love heals the wound which love has caused, and by each application renders it greater. The healing which love brings is to wound again what was wounded before, until the soul melts away in the fire of love. So when

the soul shall become wholly one wound of love it will then be transformed in love, wounded with love. For herein he who is most wounded is the most healthy, and he who is all wound is all health.

8. And yet even if the whole soul be one wound, and consequently sound, the divine burning is not intermitted; it continues its work, which is to wound the soul with love. But then, too, its work is to soothe the healed wound, and the soul therefore cries out, 'O delicious wound', and so much the more delicious the more penetrating the fire of love. The Holy Ghost inflicted the wound that he might soothe it, and as his will and desire to soothe it are great, great will be the wound which he will inflict, in order that the soul he has wounded may be greatly comforted. O blessed wound inflicted by him who cannot but heal it!

9. O happy and most blessed wound! For thou art inflicted only for the joy and comfort of the soul. Great is the wound, because he is great who has wrought it; and great is the delight of it: for the fire of love is infinite. O delicious wound then, and the more delicious the more the burn of love penetrates the inmost substance of the soul, burning all it can burn that it may supply all the delight it can give. This burning and wound, in my opinion, are the highest condition attainable in this life. There are many other forms of this burning, but they do not reach so far, neither are they like unto this: for this is the touch of the Divinity without form or figure, either natural, formal or imaginary.

10. But the soul is burned in another and most excellent way, which is this: when a soul is on fire with love, but not in the degree of which I am now speaking – though it should be so, that it may be the subject of this – it will feel as if a seraph with a burning brand of love had struck it, and penetrated it already on fire as glowing coal, or rather as a flame, and burns it utterly.[6] And then in that burn

the flame rushes forth and surges vehemently as in a glowing furnace or forge; the fire revives and the flame ascends when the burning fuel is disturbed. Then when the burning brand touches it, the soul feels that the wound it has thus received is delicious beyond all imagination. For beside being altogether moved or stirred, at the time of this stirring of the fire, by the vehement movement of the seraph, wherein the ardour and the melting of love is great, it feels that its wound is perfect, and that the herbs which serve to temper the steel are efficacious; it feels the very depths of the spirit pierced through, and its delight to be exquisite beyond the power of language to express. The soul feels, as it were, a most minute grain of mustard seed, most pungent and burning in the inmost heart of the spirit; in the spot of the wound, where the substance and the power of the herb reside, diffuse itself most subtly through all the spiritual veins of the soul in proportion to the strength and power of the heat. It feels its love to grow, strengthen and refine itself to such a degree as to seem to itself as if seas of fire were in it filling it with love.

11. The fruition of the soul now cannot be described otherwise than by saying that it understands why the kingdom of heaven is compared in the gospel to a mustard seed, which by reason of its great natural heat grows into a lofty tree. 'The kingdom of heaven is like a grain of mustard seed, which a man took and sowed in his field. Which is the least surely of all seeds; but when it is grown up, it is greater than all herbs, and is made a tree, so that the fowls of the air come and dwell in the branches thereof' (Matt. 13.31–32). The soul beholds itself now as one immense sea of fire. Few souls, however, attain to this state, but some have done so, especially those whose spirit and power is to be transmitted to their spiritual children; since God bestows on the founder gifts and graces, according to the succession of the order in the first fruits of the Spirit.

12. To return to the work of the seraph, which in truth is to strike and wound. If the effect of the wound be permitted to flow exteriorly into the bodily senses, an effect corresponding to the interior wound itself will manifest itself without. Thus it was with St Francis, for when the seraph wounded his soul with love, the effects of that wound became outwardly visible. God confers no favours on the body which he does not confer in the first place chiefly on the soul. In that case, the greater the joy and violence of the love which is the cause of the interior wound, the greater will be the pain of the visible wound, and as the former grows so does the latter.

13. The reason is this: such souls as these, being already purified and strong in God, their spirit, strong and sound, delights in the strong and sweet Spirit of God, who, however, causes pain and suffering in their weak and corruptible flesh. It is thus a most marvellous thing to feel pain and sweetness together. Job felt it when he said, 'Returning, thou tormentest me wonderfully' (Job 10.16). This is marvellous, worthy the multitude of the sweetness of God, which he has hidden for them that fear him (Ps. 31.20); the greater the sweetness and delight, the greater the pain and suffering.

14. O Infinite greatness, in all things showing thyself omnipotent. Who, O Lord, can cause sweetness in the midst of bitterness and pleasure in the midst of pain? O delicious wound, the greater the delight the deeper the wound. But when the wound is within the soul, and not communicated to the body without, it is then much more intense and keen. As the flesh is bridle to the spirit, so, when the graces of the latter overflow into the former, the flesh draws in and restrains the swift steed of the spirit and checks its course; 'for the corruptible body is a load upon the soul, and the earthly habitation presseth down the mind that museth upon many things'

(Wisd. 9.15). He, therefore, who shall trust much to the bodily senses will never become a very spiritual man.

15. This I say for the sake of those who think they can ascend to the heights and power of the spirit, by the mere energy and action of the senses, which are mean and vile. We cannot become spiritual unless the bodily sense be restrained. It is a state of things wholly different from this, when the spirit overflows into the senses, for there may be great spirituality in this; as in the case of St Paul, whose deep sense of the sufferings of Christ overflowed into his body, so that he said, 'I bear the marks of our Lord Jesus in my body' (Gal. 6.17). Thus, as the wound and the burn, so the hand that inflicted it; and as the touch, so he who touched. 'O tender hand, O gentle touch.'

'O tender hand! O gentle touch!'

16. O hand, as generous as thou art powerful and rich, giving me gifts with power. O gentle hand, laid so gently upon me, and yet, if thou wert to press at all, the whole world must perish; for only at the sight of thee the earth trembles (Ps. 104.32), the nations melt, and the mountains are crushed in pieces (Hab. 3.6). O gentle hand, I say it again, for him thou didst touch so sharply. Upon me thou art laid so softly, so lovingly and so tenderly; thou art the more gentle and sweet for me than thou wert hard for him; the loving sweetness with which thou art laid upon me is greater than the severity with which he was touched. Thou killest, and thou givest life, and there is no one who shall escape out of thy hand.

17. But thou, O divine life, never killest but to give life, as thou never woundest but to heal. Thou hast wounded me, O divine hand, that thou mayest heal me. Thou hast slain in me that which made me dead and without the life of God which I now live. This thou hast wrought in the liberality of thy gracious generosity, through that

touch, wherewith thou dost touch me, of the brightness of thy glory and the figure of thy substance (Heb. 1.3), thine only begotten Son, in whom being thy Wisdom, thou reachest 'from end to end mightily' (Wisd. 8.1).

18. O gentle, subtle touch, the Word, the Son of God, who, because of the pureness of thy divine nature, dost penetrate subtly the very substance of my soul, and, touching it gently, absorbest it wholly in divine ways of sweetness not 'heard of in the land of Canaan', nor 'seen in Teman' (Baruch 3.22). O touch of the Word, so gentle, so wonderfully gentle to me; and yet thou wert 'overthrowing mountains, and breaking rocks in Horeb', by the shadow of thy power going before, when thou didst announce thy presence to the prophet in 'the whisper of a gentle air' (1 Kings 19.11–12). O soft air, how is it that thou touchest so softly when thou art so terrible and so strong? O blessed soul, most blessed, which thou, who art so terrible and so strong, touchest so gently. Proclaim it to the world, O my soul – no, proclaim it not, for the world knoweth not the 'gentle air', neither will it listen to it, because it cannot comprehend matters so deep.

19. O my God and my life, they shall know thee (John 14.17) and behold thee when thou touchest them, who, making themselves strangers upon earth, shall purify themselves, because purity corresponds with purity. The more gently thou touchest, the more thou art hidden in the purified soul of those who have made themselves strangers here, hidden from the face of all creatures, and whom 'thou shalt hide in the secret of thy face from the disturbance of men' (Ps. 31.20).

20. O, again and again, gentle touch, which by the power of its tenderness undoest the soul, removest it far away from every touch whatever, and makest it thine own; thou which leavest behind thee effects and impressions so pure, that the touch of everything else seems vile and low, the very sight offensive, and all relations therewith

a deep affliction. The more subtle any matter is, the more it spreads and fills, and the more it diffuses itself the more subtle it is. O gentle touch, the more subtle the more infused. And now the vessel of my soul, because thou hast touched it, is pure and clean and able to receive thee.

21. O gentle touch, as in thee there is nothing material, so thy touch is the more penetrating, changing what in me is human into divine, for thy divine essence, wherewith thou touchest me, is wholly unaffected by modes and manner, free from the husks of form and figure. Finally then, O gentle touch, and most gentle, for thou touchest me with thy most simple and pure essence, which being infinite is infinitely gentle; therefore it is that this touch is so subtle, so loving, so deep and so delicious.

'Savouring of everlasting life'

22. What the soul tastes now in this touch of God is, in truth, though not perfectly, a certain foretaste of everlasting life, as I said before.[7] It is not incredible that it should be so when we believe, as we do believe, that this touch is most substantial, and that the substance of God touches the substance of the soul. Many saints have experienced it in this life. The sweetness of delight which this touch occasions baffles all description. Neither will I speak of it, lest men should suppose that it is nothing beyond what my words imply, for there are no terms by which we can designate or explain the deep things of God transacted in perfect souls. The proper way to speak of them is for him who has been favoured with them to understand them, feel them and enjoy them, and be silent.

23. For the soul now sees that they are in some measure like the white counter of which it is written 'To him that overcometh I will give . . . a white counter, and in the counter a new name written,

which no man knoweth but he that receiveth it' (Rev. 2.17). Thus it may be truly said, 'savouring of everlasting life'. For though the fruition of it is not perfect in this life as it will be in glory, nevertheless the touch, being of God, savoureth of everlasting life, and accordingly the soul tastes in a marvellous manner, and by participation, of all the things of God: fortitude, wisdom, love, beauty, grace and goodness being communicated unto it.

24. Now as God is all this, the soul tastes of all in one single touch of God in a certain eminent way. And from this good bestowed upon the soul, some of the unction of the Spirit overflows at times into the body itself, penetrating into the very bones, as it is written, 'All my bones shall say: Lord, who is like unto thee?' (Ps. 35.10). But as all I can say falls short of the subject, it is enough to repeat, 'savouring of everlasting life.'

'And paying the whole debt'

25. But what debts are they to which the soul here refers, and which it declares to be paid or satisfied ? We should know that souls which attain to this high state, to the kingdom of the spiritual betrothal, have in general passed through many tribulations and trials, because it is 'through many tribulations that we enter into the kingdom of heaven' (Acts 14.21). And these tribulations are now passed.

26. What they have to suffer who are to attain unto union with God are sundry afflictions and temptations of sense, trials, tribulations, temptations, darkness and distress of mind, so that both the flesh and the spirit may be purified together, as I said in the *Dark Night* in my treatise of the *Ascent of Mount Carmel*. The reason is that the joy and knowledge of God cannot be established in the soul, if the flesh and spirit are not perfectly purified and spiritualized, and as trials and penances purify and refine the senses, as tribulations,

temptations, darkness and distress spiritualize and prepare the spirit, so they must undergo them who would be transformed in God – as the souls in purgatory who through that trial attain to the beatific vision – some more intensely than others, some for a longer, others for a shorter time, according to those degrees of union to which God intends to raise them, and according to their need of purification.

27. It is by these trials to which God subjects the spirit and the flesh that the soul, in bitterness, acquires virtues and fortitude and perfection, as the Apostle writes, 'Power is made perfect in infirmity' (2 Cor. 12.9); for virtue is made perfect in weakness, and refined by sufferings. Iron cannot be fashioned according to the pattern of the skilled craftsman but by fire and the hammer, and during the process its previous condition is injured. This is the way in which God taught Jeremiah: 'From on high he hath cast a fire in my bones and hath taught me' (Lam. 1.13). The prophet speaks of the hammer also when he saith, 'Thou hast chastised me, and I am taught' (Jer. 31.18). So, too, the wise man asks, 'He that hath not been proved, what knoweth he?' (Ecclus. 34.10).

28. Here comes the question, why is it that so few ever attain to this state? The reason is that, in this marvellous work which God himself begins, so many are weak, shrinking from trouble and unwilling to endure the least discomfort or mortification, or to labour with constant patience. Hence it is that God, not finding them diligent in cultivating the graces he has given them when he began to try them, proceeds no further with their purification, neither does he lift them up out of the dust of the earth, because it required greater courage and resolution for this than they possessed.

29. Thus it may be said to those who desire to advance, but who will not endure a lighter trial nor submit themselves thereto, in the

words of Jeremiah, 'If with running with footmen thou hast laboured how canst thou contend with horses? And whereas in a land of peace thou hast been secure, what wilt thou do in the pride of Jordan?' (Jer. 12.5). That is, if the ordinary trials of human life to which all men living are liable are wearisome and a burden for thee, how art thou to 'contend with horses'? That is, how canst thou venture out of the common trials of life upon others of greater violence and swiftness? If thou hast been unwilling to make war against the peace and pleasures of the earth, thine own sensuality, but rather seekest comfort and tranquillity on it, what wilt thou do in the pride of Jordan? That is, how wilt thou stand against the rushing waters of tribulations and the more interior trials of the spirit?

30. O souls that seek your own ease and comfort, if you knew how necessary for this high state is suffering, and how profitable suffering and mortification are for attaining to these great blessings, you would never seek for comfort anywhere, but you would rather take up the cross with the vinegar and the gall, and would count it an inestimable favour, knowing that by thus dying to the world and to your own selves, you would live to God in spiritual joy; in the patient endurance of your exterior afflictions you would merit at the hands of God, that he should look upon you, cleanse and purify you more and more in these spiritual tribulations. They whom he thus blesses must have served him well and long, must have been patient and persevering, and their life most pleasing in his sight. The angel said unto Tobit, 'Because thou wast acceptable to God, it was necessary that temptation should prove thee' (Tobit 12.13). Tobit was acceptable to God, therefore he tried him; he gave him the grace of tribulation, the source of greater graces still, and it is written of him that 'the rest of his life was in joy' (Tobit 14.4).

31. The same truth is exemplified in the life of Job. God acknowledged him as his faithful servant in the presence of the angels good and evil, and immediately sent him heavy trials, that he might afterwards raise him higher, as he did, both in temporal and spiritual things (Job 1.8–20).

32. This is the way God deals with those whom it is his will to exalt. He suffers them to be tempted, afflicted, tormented and chastened, inwardly and outwardly, to the utmost limit of their strength, that he may deify them, unite them to himself in his wisdom, which is the highest state, purifying them, first in that wisdom, as David observed, saying that the 'words of our Lord are chaste words, silver, examined by fire', tested in the earth of our flesh and purified (Ps. 12.6) seven times, that is, made perfectly pure.

33. It is not necessary I should stop here to say how each of these purgations tends to the divine wisdom, which in this life is as silver, for however pure it may be, yet is not comparable to the pure gold, which is reserved for everlasting glory.

34. But it is very necessary for the soul to endure these tribulations and trials, inward and outward, spiritual and corporal, great and small, with great resolution and patience, accepting all as from the hand of God for its healing and its good, not shrinking from them, because they are for the health of the soul. 'If the spirit of him that hath power', saith the wise man, 'ascend upon thee, leave not thy place, because carefulness' – that is, healing – 'will make the greatest sins to cease' (Eccles. 10.4). 'Leave not thy place', that is, the place of thy trial, which is thy troubles; for the healing which they bring will break the thread of thy sins and imperfections, which is evil habits, so that they shall proceed no further. Thus, interior trials and tribulations destroy and purge away the imperfect and evil habits of the soul. We are, therefore, to count it a great favour when our Lord sends us

interior and exterior trials, remembering that they are few in number who deserve to be made perfect through sufferings so as to attain to so high a state as this.

35. I return to the explanation of the words before me. The soul now remembers that its past afflictions are most abundantly recompensed, for 'as the darkness so also the light thereof' (Ps. 139.12), and that having once been 'a partaker of the sufferings', it is now 'of the consolation' (2 Cor. 1.7), that its interior and exterior trials have been recompensed by the divine mercies, none of them being without its corresponding reward. It therefore acknowledges itself perfectly satisfied, and says, 'paying the whole debt', as David did, 'How great tribulations hast thou shown me, many and evil, and turning thou hast quickened me, and from the depths of the earth thou hast brought me back again. Thou hast multiplied thy magnificence, and turning to me thou hast comforted me' (Ps. 71.20).

36. Thus the soul which once stood without at the gates of the palace of God – like Mordecai weeping in the streets of Susa because his life was threatened, clothed with sackcloth and refusing the garments which Esther sent him, unrewarded for his faithful service in defending the king's honour and life (Esth. 4.1–6) – finds, also, like Mordecai, all its trials and service rewarded in one day. It is not only admitted within the palace and stands in royal robes before the king, but has also a diadem on its head, and in its hand a sceptre, and sitting on the royal throne with the king's signet on its finger, symbols of its power in the kingdom of the Bridegroom. For those souls who attain to this high state obtain all their desires; the whole debt is amply paid: the appetites, their enemies which sought their life, are dead, while they are living in God. 'In destroying death thou hast changed it into life.'

'Thou hast changed death into life'

37. Death is nothing else but the privation of life, for when life cometh there is no trace of death in that which is spiritual. There are two kinds of life, one beatific, consisting in the vision of God, and this must be preceded by a natural and bodily death, as it is written, 'We know if our earthly house of this habitation be dissolved, that we have a building of God, a house not made with hands, eternal in heaven' (2 Cor. 5.1). The other is the perfect spiritual life, consisting in the possession of God by the union of love. Men attain to this through the mortification of their evil habits and desires. Until this be done, the perfection of the spiritual life of union with God is unattainable. 'For,' as the Apostle saith, 'if you live according to the flesh, you shall die: but if by the spirit you mortify the deeds of the flesh, you shall live' (Rom. 8.13).

38. By 'death' here is meant the old man, that is, the employment of our faculties, memory, understanding and will upon the things of this world, and the desire on the pleasure which created things supply. All this is the old life; it is the death of the new life which is spiritual, and which the soul cannot live perfectly unless to the old man it be perfectly dead, for so the Apostle teaches, when he bids us put 'away according to the old conversation, the old man . . . and put on the new man, which, according to God, is created in justice and holiness of the truth' (Eph. 4.22, 24). In this new life, when the soul shall have attained to perfect union with God, all its affections, powers and acts, in themselves imperfect and vile, become as it were divine. And as everything that lives, to use the expression of philosophers, lives in its acts, so the soul, having its acts in God by virtue of its union with him, lives the life of God, its death being changed into life.

39. This is so, because the understanding, which, previous to its union with God, understood but dimly by means of its natural light, is now under the influence and direction of another principle, and of a higher illumination of God. The will, which previously loved but weakly, is now changed into the life of divine love, for now it loves deeply with the affections of divine love, moved by the Holy Ghost in whom it now lives. The memory, which once saw nothing but the forms and figures of created things, is now changed, and keeps in 'mind the eternal years' (Ps. 77.5), as David spoke. The desire, which previously longed for created food, now tastes and relishes the food that is divine, influenced by another and more efficacious principle, the sweetness of God.

40. Finally, all the motions and acts of the soul, proceeding from the principle of its natural and imperfect life, are now changed in this union with God into motions divine. For the soul, as the true child of God, is moved by the Spirit of God, as it is written, 'Whosoever are led by the Spirit of God, they are the sons of God' (Rom. 8.14). The substance of the soul, though it is not the substance of God, because inconvertible into him, yet being united to him and absorbed in him, is by participation God. This is accomplished in the perfect state of the spiritual life, but not so perfectly as in the other; hence is it well said: 'While slaying thou hast changed death into life.'

41. The soul, therefore, has good reason for saying with St Paul, 'I live, now not I, but Christ liveth in me' (Gal. 2.20). What in the soul is dead and cold becomes changed into the life of God, the soul 'swallowed up of life' (2 Cor. 5.4) in fulfilling the words of the Apostle, 'Death is swallowed up in victory' (1 Cor. 15.54), and those of Hosea, 'I will be thy death, O death' (Hos. 13.14).

42. The soul being thus swallowed up of life, detached from all secular and temporal things, and delivered from the disorderliness

of nature, is led into the chamber of the King, where it rejoices and is glad in the Beloved, remembering his breasts more than wine, and saying, 'I am black but beautiful, O ye daughters of Jerusalem' (Song of Songs 1.5), for my natural blackness is changed into the beauty of the heavenly King. O then, the burning of the fire, infinitely burning above all other fires, O how infinitely beyond all other fires dost thou burn me, and the more thou burnest the sweeter thou art to me. 'O delicious wound', more delicious to me than all the delights and health of the world. 'O tender hand', infinitely more tender than all tenderness, and the greater the pressure of it the more tender is it to me. 'O gentle touch', the gentleness of which surpasses infinitely all the gentleness and all the loveliness of created things, sweeter and more delicious than honey and the honeycomb, because thou savourest of everlasting life; and is the more sweet the more profoundly thou dost touch me. Thou art infinitely more precious than gold and precious stones, for thou payest debts which nothing else can pay, because thou changest marvellously death into life.

43. In this state of life, so perfect, the soul is, as it were, keeping a perpetual feast with the praises of God in its mouth, with a new song of joy and love, full of the knowledge of its high dignity. It sometimes exulteth, repeating the words of Job, 'My glory shall always be renewed', and 'as a palm tree' I 'will multiply days' (Job 29.18, 20). That is, God will not suffer my glory to grow old as before, and he will multiply my days, that is, my merits, unto heaven, as a palm tree multiplies its branches. And also the words of David in the thirtieth psalm, the soul sings interiorly to God, especially the conclusion thereof: 'Thou hast turned my mourning into joy unto me: thou hast cut my sackcloth and hast compassed me with gladness, that my glory may sing to thee, and I be not conscience-stricken' – for this

state is inaccessible to pain – 'Lord my God, for ever will I confess to thee' Ps. 30.11–12).

44. Here the soul is so conscious of God's solicitude to comfort it, feeling that he is himself encouraging it with words so precious, so tender, so endearing; that he is conferring graces upon it, one upon another, so that it seems as if there were no other soul in the world for him to comfort, no other object of his care, but that everything was done for this one soul alone. This truth is admitted by the bride in the Canticle when she says, 'My Beloved to me and I to him' (Song of Songs 2.16).

Stanza 3

O lamps of fire,
In the splendours of which
The deep caverns of sense,
Dim and dark,
With unwonted brightness
Give light and warmth together to the Beloved.

Explanation

I stand greatly in need of the help of God to enter into the deep meaning of this stanza. Great attention also is necessary on the part of the reader, for if he be without experience of the matter he will find it very obscure, while, on the other hand, it will be clear and full of sweetness to him who has had that experience.

2. In this stanza the soul most heartily thanks the Bridegroom for the great mercies which, in the state of union, it has received at his hands, for he has given therein a manifold and most profound knowledge of himself, which enlightens its powers and senses, and fills them with love. These powers, previous to the state of union, were in darkness and blindness, but are now illumined by the fires of love and respond thereto, offering that very light and love to him who has kindled and inspired them by infusing into the soul gifts so divine. For he who truly loves is satisfied then when his whole self, all he is, all he can be, all he has, and all he can acquire, is spent in the

service of his love; and the greater that service the greater is his pleasure in giving it. Such is the joy of the soul now, because it can shine in the presence of the Beloved in the splendours with which he has surrounded it, and love him with that love which he has communicated to it.

'O lamps of fire'

3. Lamps have two properties, that of giving light and of burning. If we are to understand this stanza, we must keep in mind that God in his one and simple essence is all the power and majesty of his attributes. He is omnipotent, wise, good, merciful, just, strong, loving; he is all the other attributes and perfections of which we have no knowledge here below. He is all this. When the soul is in union with him, and he is pleased to admit it to a special knowledge of himself, the soul sees in him all these perfections and majesty together in the one and simple essence clearly and distinctly, so far as it is consistent with the faith, and as each one of these attributes is the very being of God, who is the Father, the Son and the Holy Ghost – as each attribute is God himself – and as God is infinite light, and infinite divine fire, it follows that each attribute gives light and burns as God himself. God therefore, according to this knowledge of him in unity, is to the soul as many lamps, because it has the knowledge of each of them, and because they minister to it the warmth of love, each in its own way, and yet all of one substance, all one lamp. This lamp is all lamps, because it gives light, and burns, in all ways.

4. The soul seeing this, the one lamp is to it as many lamps, for though but one, it can do all things, and has all power and comprehends every spirit. And thus it may be said that the one lamp shines and burns many ways in one: it shines and burns as omnipotent, as wise, as good, ministering to the soul knowledge and love, and

revealing itself unto it, according to the measure of its strength for the reception of all. The splendour of the lamp as omnipotent gives to the soul the light and warmth of the love of God as omnipotent, and accordingly God is now the lamp of omnipotence to the soul, shining and burning according to that attribute. The splendour of the lamp as wisdom produces the warmth of the love of God as all wise, and so of the other attributes; for the light which emanates from each of the attributes of God and from all the others, produces in the soul the fire of the love of God as such. Thus God is to the soul in these communications and manifestations of himself – they are, I think, the highest possible in this life – as innumerable lamps from which light and love proceed.

5. These lamps revealed him to Moses on Mount Sinai, where God passed before him, and where Moses fell prostrate on the earth in all haste. He mentions some of the perfections of God which he then saw, and, loving him in them, speaks of them separately in the following words: 'O Lord God, merciful and clement, patient and of much compassion, and true, who keepest mercy unto thousands; who takest away iniquity and wicked deeds and sin, and no man of himself is innocent before thee' (Exod. 34.6–7). It appears that the principal attributes of God which Moses then recognized and loved were those of omnipotence, dominion, mercy, justice and truth, which was a most profound knowledge, and the deepest delight of love.

6. It follows from this that the joy and rapture of love communicated to the soul in the fire of the light of these lamps is admirable and immeasurable: as abundant as from many lamps, each of which burns with love, the heat of one subserving that of the other, as the light of one ministers to that of the other; all of them forming but one light and fire, and each of them that one fire. The soul, too, infinitely absorbed in these delicious flames, is subtly wounded by

each one of them, and by all of them more subtly and more profoundly, in the love of life; the soul sees clearly that this love is
everlasting life, which is the union of all blessings, and recognizes
the truth of those words, 'The lamps thereof lamps of fire and flames'
(Song of Songs 8.6).

7. If 'a great and darksome horror seized upon' Abram as he saw
one 'lamp of fire passing' before him (Gen. 15.12, 17), when he learned
with what rigorous justice God was about to visit the Canaanites
shall not the lamps of the knowledge of God shining now sweetly
and lovingly produce greater light and joy of love than that one lamp
produced of horror and darkness, when it passed before Abram?
O my soul! how great, how excellent and how manifold will be thy
light and joy: seeing that in all, and by all, thou shalt feel that
he gives thee his own joy and love, loving thee according to his
powers, attributes and properties. For he who loves and does good
to another honours him and does him good according to his own
nature and qualities. Thus the Bridegroom abiding in thee, being
all-powerful, gives himself to thee, and loves thee with all power;
being wise, with wisdom; being good, with goodness; being holy, with
holiness. And as he is liberal thou wilt feel also that he loves thee
with liberality, without self-interest, only to do thee good, showing
joyfully his countenance full of grace, and saying: I am thine and for
thee, and it is my pleasure to be what I am, that I may give myself
to thee and be thine.

8. Who then shall describe thy feeling, O blessed soul, when thus
beloved, and so highly honoured? 'Thy belly as a heap of wheat compassed about with lilies' (Song of Songs 7.2). 'Thy belly', that is, thy
will, is like a heap of wheat covered and compassed with lilies; for
in the grains of wheat which form the bread of life, which thou now
art tasting, the lilies of virtue, which gird thee about, fill thee with

delight. For the daughters of the king, that is, the virtues, will delight thee wondrously with the fragrance of their aromatic herbs, which are the knowledge of himself which he gives thee. Thou wilt be so absorbed in this knowledge, and it will be so infused in thee that thou shalt be also 'a well of living waters which run with a strong stream from Mount Libanus' (Song of Songs 4.15), and Libanus is God. Thy joy will now be so marvellously complete, because the words of the Psalmist are accomplished in thee: 'The violence of the river maketh the city of God joyful' (Ps. 46.4).

9. O wonder! The soul is now overflowing with the divine waters, which run from it as from an abundant fountain unto everlasting life (John 4.14). It is true that this communication is light and fire of the lamps of God, yet the fire is here so sweet that, though an infinite fire, it is as the waters of life which satisfy the soul, and quench its thirst with that vehemence for which the spirit longs. Thus, though they are lamps of fire, they are also the living waters of the spirit. Those which descended on the Apostles, though lamps of fire, were also waters pure and limpid, according to the words of Ezekiel who thus prophesied the descent of the Holy Ghost: 'I will pour out upon you clean water, and will put a new spirit in the midst of you' (Ezek. 36.25–26). Thus though it be fire, it is water also, a figure of which we have in the sacrificial fire, hid by Jeremiah (2 Macc. 2.1), it was water in the place of concealment, but fire when it was brought forth and sprinkled upon the sacrifice (2 Macc. 1.22).

10. So in like manner the Spirit of God, while hidden in the veins of the soul, is sweet water quenching its spiritual thirst; but when the soul offers the sacrifice of love, the Spirit is then living flames of fire, and these are the lamps of the acts of love which the bride spoke of in the Canticle when she said, 'The lamps thereof lamps of fire and flames' (Song of Songs 8.6). The soul speaks of them thus because

it has the fruition thereof not only as waters of wisdom, but also as the fire of love in an act of love, saying, 'O lamps of fire'. All language now is ineffectual to express the matter. If we consider that the soul is now transformed in God, we shall in some measure understand how it is true that it is also become a fountain of living waters boiling and bubbling upwards in the fire of love which is God.

'In the splendours'

11. I have already said that these splendours are the communications of the divine lamps in which the soul in union shines with its powers, memory, understanding and will, enlightened and united in this loving knowledge. But we are not to suppose that the light of these splendours is like that of material fire, when it breaks into flames and heats objects external to it, but rather when it heats what is within it, for the soul is now within these splendours – 'in the splendours'. That is to say, it is within them, not near them, within their splendours, in the flames of the lamps, itself transformed in flame.

12. The soul therefore may be said to resemble the air which is burning within the flame and transformed in fire, for the flame is nothing else but air inflamed. The flickerings of the flame are not those of air only or of fire only, but of air and fire together; and the fire causes the air which is within to burn. It is thus that the soul with its powers is illumined in the splendours of God. The movements of the flame, that is its vibrations and its flickerings, are not the work of the soul only, transformed in the fire of the Holy Ghost, nor of the Holy Ghost only, but of the soul and of the Holy Ghost together who moves the soul as the fire moves the air that is burning.

13. Thus, then, these movements of God and of the soul together are as it were the acts of God by which he renders the soul glorious.

For these vibrations and movements are the 'playing' and the joyous feasts of the Holy Ghost in the soul, spoken of before,[8] in which he seems to be on the point of admitting it into everlasting life. And thus these movements and quiverings of the flame are as it were goads applied to the soul, furthering its translation into his perfect glory now that it is really entered into him. So with fire: all movements and vibrations which it makes in the air burning within it are efforts to ascend to its proper sphere, and that as quickly as possible, but they are all fruitless because the air itself is within its own sphere.

14. In the same way the movements of the Holy Ghost, though full of fire and most effectual to absorb the soul in great bliss, do not accomplish their work until the time is come when it is to sally forth from the sphere of the air of this mortal life and reach the centre of the spirit, the perfect life in Christ. These visions of the glory of God, to which the soul is now admitted, are more continuous than they used to be, more perfect and more stable; but in the life to come they will be most perfect, unchanging and uninterrupted. There, too, the soul will see clearly how that God, though here appearing to move within it, yet in himself moves not at all, as the fire moves not in its sphere. These splendours are inestimable graces and favours which God bestows upon the soul. They are called also overshadowings, and are, in my opinion, the greatest and the highest graces which can be bestowed in this life in the way of transformation.

15. Now overshadowing is the throwing of a shadow; and to throw one's shadow over another signifies protection and favour, for when the shadow of one touches us, it is a sign that he whose shadow it is stands by us to favour and protect us. Thus it was said to the Virgin, 'The power of the Most High shall overshadow thee' (Luke 1.35), for the Holy Ghost was about to approach her so closely as to 'come

upon' her. The shadow of every object partakes of the nature and proportions of it, for if the object be dense, the shadow will be dense and dark; if it be light and clear, so will be the shadow, as we see in the case of wood or crystal: the former being dense, throws a dark shadow, and the latter being clear, throws a shadow that is light. In spiritual things, too, death is the privation of all things, so the shadow of death will be darkness, which in a manner deprives us of all things. Thus, too, speaks the Psalmist, saying, 'sitting in darkness and the shadow of death' (Ps. 107.10), whether the spiritual darkness of spiritual death, or the bodily darkness of bodily death.

16. The shadow of life is light, if divine, a divine light, and if the shadow be human, the light is natural, and so the shadow of beauty will be as another beauty according to the nature and properties of that beauty of which it is the shadow. The shadow of strength will be as another strength, in measure and proportion. The shadow of wisdom will be another wisdom, or rather, beauty, strength and wisdom themselves will be in the shadow, wherein is traced the form and property, the shadow whereof is there.

17. This, then, being so, what must be the shadow of the Holy Ghost, the shadow of all his power, might and attributes, when he is so near the soul? He touches the soul not with his shadow only, for he unites himself to it, feeling and tasting with it the form and attributes of God in the shadow of God: that is, feeling and tasting the property of divine power in the shadow of omnipotence: feeling and tasting the divine wisdom in the shadow of the divine wisdom: and finally, tasting the glory of God in the shadow of glory, which begets the knowledge and the taste of the property and form of the glory of God. All this takes place in clear and luminous shadows, because the attributes and powers of God are lamps, which, being resplendent and luminous in their own nature, throw forth shadows

resplendent and luminous, and a multitude of them in one sole essence.

18. O what a vision for the soul when it shall experience the power of that which Ezekiel saw: 'the likeness of four living creatures', and the 'wheel with four faces', the appearance 'like that of burning coals of fire, and like the appearance of lamps' (Ezek. 1.5, 13, 15), when it shall behold that wheel, the wisdom of God, full of eyes within and without, that is the marvellous knowledge of wisdom; when it shall hear the noise of their wings as they pass, a noise 'like the noise of an army', that is, of many things at once which the soul learns by one sole sound of God's passing before it; and finally, when it shall hear the beating of the wings, which is like the 'noise of many waters, as it were the voice of the Most High God' (Ezek. 1.24), which signifies the rushing of the divine waters, the overflowing of which on the descent of the Holy Ghost envelops the soul in a flame of love. Here the soul rejoices in the glory of God, under the protection of his shadow, for the prophet adds: 'This was the vision of the likeness of the glory of our Lord' (Ezek. 1.28). O the height to which this blessed soul is raised! O how exalted! O how it marvels at the visions it has within the limits of the faith! Who can describe them? O how it is profoundly immersed in these waters of the divine splendours where the everlasting Father is pouring forth the irrigating streams with a bounteous hand, for these streams penetrate soul and body.

19. O wonder! The lamps of the divine attributes, though one in substance, are still distinct, each burning as the other, one being substantially the other. O abyss of delights, and the more abundant, the more their riches are gathered together in infinite simplicity and unity. There each one is so recognized and felt as not to hinder the feeling and recognition of the other; yea, rather everything in thee is light which does not impede anything; and by reason of thy

pureness, O divine Wisdom, many things are known in thee in one, for thou art the treasury of the everlasting Father, 'the brightness of eternal light, the unspotted mirror of God's majesty, and the image of his goodness' (Wisd. 7.26), 'in the splendours'.

'The deep caverns of sense'

20. The caverns are the powers of the soul, memory, understanding and will, and their depth is commensurate with their capacity for great good, because nothing less than the infinite can fill them. What they suffer when they are empty shows in some measure the greatness of their delight when they are full of God; for contraries are known by contraries. In the first place, it is to be remembered that these caverns are not conscious of their extreme emptiness when they are not purified and cleansed from all affection for created things. In this life every trifle that enters them is enough to perplex them, to render them insensible to their loss, and unable to recognize the infinite good which is wanting, or their own capacity for it. It is assuredly a most wonderful thing how, notwithstanding their capacity for infinite good, a mere trifle perplexes them, so that they cannot become the recipients of that for which they are intended, till they are completely emptied.

21. But when they are empty and cleansed, the hunger, the thirst and the anxiety of the spiritual sense become intolerable, for as the appetite of these caverns is large, so their suffering is great, because the food which they need is great, namely, God. This feeling of pain, so deep, usually occurs towards the close of the illumination and the purgation of the soul, previous to the state of perfect union, during which it is satisfied. For when the spiritual appetite is empty, pure from every creature and from every affection thereto, and when the natural temper is lost and the soul tempered to the divine, and the

emptied appetite is well disposed – the divine communication in the union with God being still withheld – the pain of this emptiness and thirst is greater than that of death, especially then when certain glimpses of the divine ray are visible, but not communicated. Souls in this state suffer from impatient love, and they cannot endure it long without either receiving that which they desire, or dying.[9]

22. As to the first cavern, which is the understanding, its emptiness is the thirst after God. So great is this thirst, that the Psalmist compares it to that of the hart, for he knew of none greater, saying, 'As the hart desireth the fountains of waters: so doth my soul desire thee, O God' (Ps. 42.1). This thirst is a thirst for the waters of the divine Wisdom, the object of the understanding. The second cavern is the will, and the emptiness thereof is a hunger so great after God that the soul faints away, as the Psalmist saith, 'My soul longeth and fainteth for the courts of our Lord' (Ps. 84.2). This hunger is for the perfection of love, the object of the soul's desires. The third cavern is the memory, and the emptiness thereof is the soul's melting away and languishing for the possession of God: 'I will be mindful and remember', saith Jeremiah, 'and my soul shall languish within me: these things I shall think over in my heart, therefore will I hope' (Lam. 3.20–21).

23. Great, then, is the capacity of these caverns, because that which they are capable of containing is great and infinite, that is, God. Thus their capacity is in a certain sense infinite, their hunger and thirst infinite also, and their languishing and their pain, in their way, infinite. So when the soul is suffering this pain, though the pain be not so keen as in the other world, it seems to be a vivid image of that pain, because the soul is in a measure prepared to receive that which fills it, the privation of which is the greatest pain. Nevertheless the suffering belongs to another condition, for it abides in the depth of

the will's love; but in this life love does not alleviate the pain, because the greater it is the greater the soul's impatience for the fruition of God, for which it hopes continually with intense desire.

24. But, O my God, seeing it is certain that when the soul truly longs for God it is already, as St Gregory saith,[10] entered into possession, how comes it that it is in pain? If the desire of the angels, of which St Peter speaks, to look upon the Son of God (1 Pet. 1.12) is free from pain and anxiety, because they have the fruition of him, it would seem then that the soul also having the fruition of God in proportion to its desire of him – and the fruition of God is the fullness of delight – must in this its desire, in proportion to its intensity, be conscious of that fullness, seeing that it longs so earnestly after God, and so herein there ought not to be any suffering or pain.

25. But it is not so, for there is a great difference between the fruition of God by grace only, and the fruition of him in union; the former is one of mutual good will, the latter one of special communion. This difference resembles that which exists between betrothal and marriage. The former implies only an agreement and consent: bridal presents, and ornaments graciously given by the bridegroom. But marriage involves also personal union and mutual self-surrender. Though in the state of betrothal, the bridegroom is sometimes seen by the bride, and gives her presents; yet there is no personal union, which is the end of betrothal.[11]

26. In the same way, when the soul has become so pure in itself, and in its powers, that the will is purged completely from all strange desires and inclinations, in its higher and lower nature, and is wholly given up to God, the will of both being one in free and ready concord, it has then attained to the fruition of God by grace in the state of betrothal and conformity of will. In this state of spiritual betrothal of the soul and the Word, the Bridegroom confers great favours upon

the soul, and visits it oftentimes most lovingly to its great comfort and delight, but not to be compared with those of the spiritual marriage.

27. Now, though it is true that this takes place in the soul when it is perfectly cleansed of every affection to creatures – because that must occur previous to the spiritual betrothal – still other positive dispositions on the part of God, his visits and gifts of greater excellence, are requisite for this union, and for the spiritual marriage. It is by means of these dispositions, gifts and visits that the soul grows more and more in purity, beauty and refinement, so as to be fittingly prepared for a union so high. All this requires time, in some souls more, in others less. We have a type of this in the history of the virgins chosen for King Ahasuerus. These were taken in all the provinces of the kingdom, and brought from their fathers' houses; but before they could be presented to the king, they were kept in the palace a whole year. For six months they were anointed with oil of myrrh, and for the other six with certain perfumes and sweet spices of a costlier nature, after which they appeared in the presence of the king (Esth. 2.2, 12).

28. During the time of the betrothal, and in expectation of the spiritual marriage in the unction of the Holy Ghost, when the unction disposing the soul for union is most penetrating, the anxieties of the caverns are wont to become most pressing and keen. For as these unctions are a proximate disposition for union with God, because most near unto him, they make the soul more eager for him, and inspire it with a keener longing after him. Thus this desire is much more keen and deep, because the desire for God is a preparation for union with him.

29. This is a good opportunity to warn souls whom God is guiding to this delicate unction to take care what they are doing, and to

whose hands they commit themselves, that they may not go backwards, were it not beside my purpose. But such is the pain and grief of heart which I feel at the sight of some souls who go backwards, not only by withdrawing themselves from the further anointing of the Holy Ghost, but by losing the effects of what they have already received, that I cannot refrain from speaking on the subject, and telling them what they ought to do in order to avoid so great a loss. I will therefore leave my subject for a moment, but I shall return to it again soon. And in truth the consideration of this matter tends to elucidate the property of these caverns, and it is also necessary, not only for those souls who prosper in their work, but also for all others who are searching after the Beloved.

30. In the first place, if a soul is seeking after God, the Beloved is seeking it much more; if it sends after him its loving desires, which are sweet as 'a pillar of smoke of aromatic spices, of myrrh and frankincense' (Song of Songs 3.6), he on his part sends forth the odour of his ointments, which draw the soul and make it run after him (Song of Songs 1.3). These ointments are his divine inspirations and touches, which, if they come from him, are always directed and ordered by the motives of perfection according to the law of God and the faith, in which perfection the soul must ever draw nearer and nearer unto God. The soul, therefore, ought to see that the desire of God in all the graces which he bestows upon it by means of the unction and odour of his ointments, is to dispose it for another and higher unction, and more in union with his nature, until it attains to that simple and pure disposition, which is meritorious of the divine union, and of its transformation in all its powers.

31. The soul, therefore, considering that God is the chief doer in this matter, that it is he who guides it and leads it by the hand whither it cannot come of itself, namely, unto supernatural things

beyond the reach of understanding, memory and will, must take especial care to put no difficulties in the way of its guide, who is the Holy Ghost, on that road along which he leads it by the law of God and the faith. Such a difficulty will be raised if the soul entrusts itself to a blind guide; and the blind guides which can lead it astray are three, namely, the spiritual director, the devil and its own self.

32. As to the first of these, it is of the greatest importance to the soul desirous of perfection and anxious not to fall back to consider well into whose hands it resigns itself; for as the master so is the disciple; as the father so the child. You will scarcely find one who is in all respects qualified to guide a soul in the higher parts of this road, or even in the ordinary divisions of it, for a director must be learned, prudent and experienced. Though the foundations of good direction be learning and discretion, yet if experience of the higher ways be wanting, there are no means of guiding a soul therein when God is showing the way, and inexperienced directors may do great harm. Such directors, not understanding these ways of the Spirit, very frequently make souls lose the unction of the delicate ointments, by means of which the Holy Ghost is preparing them for himself: they are guiding them by other means of which they have read, but which are adapted only for beginners. These directors, knowing how to guide beginners only – and God grant they may know that – will not suffer their penitents to advance, though it be the will of God, beyond the mere rudiments, acts of reflection and imagination, whereby their progress is extremely little.[12]

33. In order to have a better knowledge of the state of beginners, we must keep in mind that it is one of meditation and of acts of reflection. It is necessary to furnish the soul in this state with matter for meditation, that it may make reflections and interior acts, and avail itself of the sensible spiritual heat and fervour, for this is

necessary in order to accustom the senses and desires to good things, that, being satisfied by the sweetness thereof, they may be detached from the world.

34. When this is in some degree effected, God begins at once to introduce the soul into the state of contemplation, and that very quickly, especially religious, because these, having renounced the world, quickly fashion their senses and desires according to God; they have therefore to pass at once from meditation to contemplation. This passage, then, takes place when the discursive acts and meditation fail, when sensible sweetness and first fervours cease, when the soul cannot make reflections as before, nor find any sensible comfort, but is fallen into aridity, because the chief matter is changed into the spirit, and the spirit is not cognizable by sense. As all the natural operations of the soul, which are within its control, depend on the senses only, it follows that God is now working in a special manner in this state, that it is he that infuses and teaches, that the soul is the recipient on which he bestows spiritual blessings by contemplation, the knowledge and the love of himself together; that is, he gives it loving knowledge without the instrumentality of its discursive acts, because it is no longer able to form them as before.

35. At this time, then, the direction of the soul must be wholly different from what it was at first. If formerly it was supplied with matter for meditation and it did meditate, now that matter must be withheld and meditation must cease because, as I have said, it cannot meditate, do what it will, and distractions are the result.[13] If before it looked for fervour and sweetness and found them, let it look for them no more nor desire them; and if it attempt to seek them, not only will it not find them, but it will meet with aridity, because it turns away from the peaceful and tranquil good secretly bestowed upon it, when it attempts to fall back on the operations of sense. In

this way it loses the latter without gaining the former, because the senses have ceased to be the channel of spiritual good.

36. Souls in this state are not to be forced to meditate or to apply themselves to discursive reflections laboriously effected, neither are they to strive after sweetness and fervour, for if they did so, they would be thereby hindering the principal agent, who is God himself, for he is now secretly and quietly infusing wisdom into the soul, together with the loving knowledge of himself, without many divers distinct or separated acts. But he produces them sometimes in the soul, and that for some space of time. The soul then must be lovingly intent upon God without distinctly eliciting other acts beyond these to which he inclines it; it must be as it were passive, making no efforts of its own, purely, simply and lovingly intent upon God, as a man who opens his eyes with loving attention. For as God is now dealing with the soul in the way of bestowing by simple and loving knowledge, so the soul also, on its part, must deal with him in the way of receiving by simple and loving knowledge, so that knowledge may be joined to knowledge, and love to love; because it is necessary here that the recipient should be adapted to the gift, and not otherwise, and that the gift may be accepted and preserved as it is given.

37. It is evident, therefore, that if the soul does not now abandon its ordinary way of meditation, it will receive this gift of God in a scanty and imperfect manner, not in that perfection with which it is bestowed; for the gift being so grand, and an infused gift, cannot be received in this scanty and imperfect way. Consequently, if the soul will at this time make efforts of its own, and encourage another disposition than that of passive loving attention, most submissive and calm, and if it does not abstain from its previous discursive acts, it will place a barrier against those graces which God is about to

communicate to it in this loving knowledge. He gives his grace to beginners in the exercise of purgation, as I have said,[14] and afterwards with an increase of the sweetness of love.

38. But if the soul is to be the recipient of his grace passively, in the natural way of God, and not in the supernatural way of the soul, it follows that, in order to be such a recipient, it must be perfectly detached, calm, peaceful and serene, as God is; it must be like the atmosphere, which the sun illumines and warms in proportion to its calmness and purity. Thus the soul must be attached to nothing, not even to meditation, not to sensible or spiritual sweetness, because God requires a spirit free and annihilated, for every act of the soul, even of thought, of liking or disliking, will hinder and disturb it, and break that profound silence of sense and spirit necessary for hearing the deep and soft voice of God, who, in the words of Hosea, speaks to the heart in solitude (Hos. 2.14); it is in profound peace and tranquillity that the soul, like David, is to listen to God, who will speak peace unto his people (Ps. 85.8). When this takes place, when the soul feels that it is silent and listens, its loving attention must be most pure, without a thought of self, in a manner self-forgotten, so that it shall be wholly intent upon hearing, for thus it is that the soul is free and ready for that which our Lord requires at its hands.

39. This tranquillity and self-forgetfulness are ever attended with a certain interior absorption; and, therefore, under no circumstances whatever, either of time or place, is it lawful for the soul, now that it has begun to enter the state of contemplation, tranquil and simple, to go back to its previous meditation, or to cleave to spiritual sweetness, as I have said, and at great length, in the tenth chapter of the first book of the *Dark Night*, and previously in the last chapter of the second, and in the first of the third book of the *Ascent of Mount Carmel*. It must detach itself from all spiritual sweetness, rise above

it in freedom of spirit; this is what the prophet Habakkuk did, for he says of himself, 'I will stand upon my watch' over my senses – that is, I will leave them below – 'and fix my step upon the munition' of my faculties – that is, they shall not advance a step even in thought – 'and I will behold to see what will be said to me' (Hab. 2.1), that is, I will receive what God shall communicate to me passively.

40. I have already said that to contemplate is to receive,[15] and it is impossible to receive the highest wisdom, that is contemplation, otherwise than in a silent spirit, detached from all sweetness and particular knowledge. So the prophet Isaiah when he says, 'Whom shall he teach knowledge? and whom shall he make to understand the thing heard? them that are weaned from the milk', that is, from sweetness and personal likings, 'that are plucked away from the breasts' (Isa. 28.9), from reliance on particular knowledge. Take away, O spiritual man, the mote and the film from thine eye, and make it clean, and then the sun will shine for thee, and thou shalt see clearly, establish thy soul in the freedom of calm peace, withdraw it from the yoke and slavery of the miserable efforts of thine own strength, which is the captivity of Egypt – for all thou canst do is little more than to gather straw for the bricks – and guide it into the land of promise flowing with milk and honey.

41. O spiritual director, remember it is for this liberty and holy rest of sons that God calls the soul into the wilderness; there it journeys in festal robes, with ornaments of gold and silver (Exod. 33.4), for the Egyptians are spoiled and their riches carried away (Exod. 12.35). Nor is this all: the enemies of the soul are drowned in the sea of contemplation, where the Egyptian of sense finds no support for his feet, leaving the child of God free, that is, the spirit, to transcend the narrow limits of its own operations, of its low views, rude perceptions and wretched likings. God does all this for the soul that he may

give it the sweet manna, which, though 'it contains all that is delicious and the sweetness of every taste' (Wisd. 16.20) – objects of desire for the soul according to thy direction – and though it is so delicious that it melts in the mouth, thy penitent shall not taste of it, if he desires anything else, for he shall not receive it.

42. Strive, therefore, to root out of the soul all desire of consolation, sweetness and meditations; do not disquiet it about spiritual things, still less about earthly things; establish it in perfect detachment, and in the utmost possible solitude. For the greater its progress in this, and the more rapidly it attains to this calm tranquillity, the more abundant will be the infusion of the spirit of divine wisdom, the loving, calm, lonely, peaceful, sweet ravisher of the spirit. The soul will feel itself at times enraptured, gently and tenderly wounded, not knowing by whom, how or when, because the Spirit communicates himself to it without effort on its part. The least work of God in the soul in this state of holy rest and solitude is an inestimable good, transcending the very thought of the soul and of its spiritual guide, and though it does not appear so then, it will show itself in due time.

43. What the soul is now conscious of is a certain estrangement and alienation from all things around it, at one time more than at another, with a certain sweet aspiration of love and life of the spirit, an inclination to solitude, and a sense of weariness in the things of this world, for when we taste of the spirit, the flesh becomes insipid. But the interior goods which silent contemplation impresses on the soul without the soul's consciousness of them are of inestimable value, for they are the most secret and delicious unctions of the Holy Ghost, whereby he secretly fills the soul with the riches of his gifts and graces; for being God, he doeth the work of God as God.

44. These goods, then, these great riches, these sublime and delicate unctions, this knowledge of the Holy Ghost, which, on account of

their exquisite and subtle pureness, neither the soul itself, nor he who directs it, can comprehend, but only he who infuses them in order to render it more pleasing to himself – are most easily, even by the slightest application of sense or desire to any particular knowledge or sweetness, disturbed and hindered. This is a serious evil, grievous and lamentable. O how sad and how wonderful! The evil done is not perceived, and the barrier raised between God and the soul is almost nothing, and yet it is more grievous, an object of deeper sorrow, and inflicts a greater stain, than any other, though seemingly more important, in common souls which have not attained to such a high state of pureness. It is as if a beautiful painting were roughly handled, besmeared with coarse and vile colours; for the injury done is greater, more observable and more deplorable than it would be if a multitude of common paintings were thus bedaubed.

45. Though this evil be so great that it cannot be exaggerated, it is still so common that there is scarcely one spiritual director who does not inflict it upon souls whom God has begun to lead by this way to contemplation. For, whenever God is anointing a soul with the unction of loving knowledge, most delicate, serene, peaceful, lonely, strange to sense and imagination; whenever he withholds all sweetness from it, and suspends its power of meditation – because he reserves it for this lonely unction, inclining it to solitude and quiet – a spiritual director will appear, who, like a rough blacksmith, knows only the use of his hammer, and who, because all his knowledge is limited to the coarser work, will say to it: Come, get rid of this, this is waste of time and idleness: arise and meditate, resume thine interior acts, for it is necessary that thou shouldest make diligent efforts of thine own; everything else is delusion and folly. Such a director as this does not understand the degrees of prayer, nor the ways of the Spirit, neither does he consider that what he

recommends the soul to do is already done, since it has passed beyond meditation and is detached from the things of sense; for when the goal is reached, and the journey ended, all further travelling must be away from the goal.

46. Such a director, therefore, is one who understands not that the soul has already attained to the life of the Spirit, wherein there is no reflection, and where the senses cease from their work; where God is himself the agent in a special way, and is speaking in secret to the solitary soul. Directors of this kind bedaub the soul with the coarse ointments of particular knowledge and sensible sweetness, to which they bring it back; they rob it of its loneliness and recollection, and consequently disfigure the exquisite work which God was doing within it. The soul that is under such guidance as this fails in one method and does not profit by the other.

47. Let spiritual directors of this kind remember that the Holy Ghost is the principal agent here, and the real guide of souls; that he never ceases to take care of them and never neglects any means by which they may profit and draw near unto God as quickly as possible, and in the best way. Let them remember that they are not the agents, but instruments only to guide souls by the rule of the faith and the law of God, according to the spirit which God gives to everyone. Their aim therefore should be not to guide souls by a way of their own suitable to themselves, but to ascertain, if they can, the way by which God himself is guiding them. If they cannot ascertain it, let them leave these souls alone and not disquiet them. Let them adapt their instructions to the direction of God, and endeavour to lead their penitents into greater solitude, liberty and tranquillity, and not fetter them when God is leading them on.

48. The spiritual director must not be anxious or afflicted because the soul is doing nothing, as he imagines, for provided the soul of

his penitent be detached from all particular knowledge, from every desire and inclination of sense; provided it abide in the self-denial of poverty of spirit, emptied of darkness and sweetness, weaned from the breast – for this is all that the soul should look to, and all that the spiritual director is to consider as within the province of them both – it is impossible – according to the course of the divine goodness and mercy – that God will not perform his own work, yea, more impossible than that the sun should not shine in a clear and cloudless sky. As the sun rising in the morning enters the house if the windows are open, so God, the unsleeping keeper of Israel (Ps. 121.4), enters the emptied soul and fills it with good things. God is, like the sun, above our souls and ready to enter within them.

49. Let spiritual directors, therefore, be content to prepare souls according to the laws of evangelical perfection, which consists in detachment, and in the emptiness of sense and spirit. Let them not go beyond this with the building, for that is the work of our Lord alone, from whom cometh 'every perfect gift' (Jas. 1.17). For, 'unless our Lord build the house, they labour in vain that build it' (Ps. 127.1). And as he is the supernatural builder, he will build up in every soul, according to his own good pleasure, the supernatural building. Do thou, who art the spiritual director, dispose the natural faculties by annihilating them in their acts – that is thy work; the work of God, as the wise man says (Prov. 16.1, 9), is to direct man's steps towards supernatural goods by ways and means utterly unknown to thee and thy penitent.

50. Say not, therefore, that thy penitent is making no progress, or is doing nothing, for if he have no greater pleasure than he once had in particular knowledge, he is advancing towards that which is above nature. Neither do thou complain that thy penitent has no distinct perceptions, for if he had he would be making no progress, because

God is incomprehensible, surpassing all understanding. And so the further the penitent advances, the further from himself must he go, walking by faith, believing and not seeing; he thus draws nearer unto God by not understanding, than by understanding. Trouble not thyself about this, for if the understanding goes not backwards occupying itself with distinct knowledge and other matters of this world, it is going forwards; for to go forwards is to go more and more by faith. The understanding, having neither the knowledge nor the power of comprehending God, advances towards him by not understanding.[16] Thus, then, what thou judgest amiss in thy penitent is for his profit: namely, that he does not perplex himself with distinct perceptions, but walks onwards in perfect faith.

51. Or, you will say, perhaps, that the will, if the understanding have no distinct perceptions, will be at the least idle, and without love, because we can love nothing that we do not know. That is true as to the natural actions of the soul, for the will does not love or desire anything of which there is no distinct conception in the understanding. But in the matter of infused contemplation, it is not at all necessary for the soul to have distinct knowledge, or to form many discursive acts, because God himself is then communicating to it loving knowledge, which is at the same time heat and light indistinctly, and then according to the state of the understanding love also is in the will. As the knowledge is general and dim – the understanding being unable to conceive distinctly what it understands – so the will also loves generally and indistinctly. For as God is light and love in this delicate communication, he informs equally the understanding and the will, though at times his presence is felt in one more than in the other. At one time the understanding is more filled with knowledge than the will with love, and at another, love is deeper than knowledge.

52. There is no reason, therefore, to be afraid of the will's idleness in this state, for if it ceases to elicit acts directed by particular knowledge, so far as they depend on itself, God inebriates it with infused love through the knowledge which contemplation ministers, as I have just said.

53. These acts of the will which are consequent upon infused contemplation are so much the nobler, the more meritorious and the sweeter, the nobler the source, God, who infuses this love and kindles it in the soul, for the will is now near unto God, and detached from other joys. Take care, therefore, to empty the will and detach it from all its inclinations, for if it is not going backwards, searching after sweetness and comfort, even though it have none in God distinctly felt, it is really advancing upwards above all such things to God, seeing that it is without any particular pleasure.

54. And though the penitent have no particular comfort in God distinctly apprehended, though he does not make distinct acts of love, he does find more comfort in him in that general secret and dim infusion than if he were under the influence of distinct acts of knowledge, because the soul sees clearly then that not one of them can furnish so much comfort and delight as this calm and lonely infusion. He loves God, too, more than all lovely things, because the soul has thrown aside all other joys and pleasures; they have become insipid.

55. There is no ground for uneasiness here, for if the will can find no rest in the joys and satisfactions of particular acts, there is then real progress, because not to go backwards, embracing what is sensible, is to go onwards to the unapproachable, who is God. Hence, then, if the will is to advance, it is to do so more by detachment from, than by attachment to, what is pleasurable and sweet. Herein is fulfilled the precept of love, namely, that we are to love him above all

things. And if this love is to be perfect, we must live in perfect detachment, and in a special emptiness of all things.

56. Neither are we to be distressed when the memory is emptied of all forms and figures; for as God is without form or figure, the memory is safe when emptied of them, and draws thereby the nearer to God. For the more the memory relies on the imagination, the further it departs from God, and the greater the risks it runs; because God, being above our thoughts, is not cognizable by the imagination. These spiritual directors, not understanding souls who have already entered into the state of quiet and solitary contemplation, because they know it not, and perhaps have never advanced beyond the ordinary state of reflection and meditation themselves, look upon the penitents, of whom I am speaking, as idle – for 'the sensual man', the man who still dwells with the feelings of the sensual part of the soul, 'perceiveth not these things that are of the Spirit of God' (1 Cor. 2.14) – disturb the peace of that calm and tranquil contemplation given them by God, and force them back to their former meditations.

57. This is followed by great loss, repugnance, dryness and distractions on the part of penitents, who desire to abide in quiet and peaceful self-recollection. These directors will have them strive after sweetness and fervour, though in truth they should have given them a wholly different advice. The penitents are unable to follow their direction, being incapable of meditating as before; because the time for that is past, and because that is not their road. They are, therefore, doubly disquieted, and imagine themselves in the way of perdition. Their directors encourage them in this supposition, dry up their spirit, rob them of the precious unctions which God gave them in solitude and calm – and this is a great evil – and furnish them with mere mud instead, for they lose the former, and labour in vain with the latter.

58. Such directors as these do not really know what spirituality is. They wrong God most grievously, and treat him irreverently, putting forth their coarse hands to the work which he is doing himself. It has cost God not a little to have brought souls thus far, and he greatly prizes this solitude to which he has led them, this emptiness of their faculties, for he has brought them thither that he may speak to their heart (Hos. 2.14), that is what he always desires. He is now taking them by the hand and reigning in them in the abundance of peace. He has deprived the discursive faculties of their strength, wherewith they had 'laboured all the night' and had taken nothing (Luke 5.5), he feeds them now in spirit, not by the operation of sense, because the senses together with their acts cannot contain the spirit.

59. How precious in his sight is this calm, or sleep, or annihilation of the senses, his words in the Canticle show: 'I adjure you, O daughters of Jerusalem, by the roes and harts of the fields, that you stir not up nor awake my beloved till she please' (Song of Songs 3.5). Those words tell us how much he loves this sleep and lonely oblivion of the soul, by the mention of those solitary and retiring animals. But the spiritual directors of whom I am speaking will not suffer their penitents to rest; they insist upon continual labour, so that God shall find no opportunity for doing his work; the work of God they undo and disfigure by the work of the soul, and the little foxes that destroy the vines are not driven away. God complains of these directors by the mouth of the prophet, saying, 'You have devoured the vineyard' (Isa. 3.14).

60. But it may be said that these directors err, perhaps, with good intentions, because their knowledge is scanty. Be it so; but they are not therefore justified in giving the rash counsels they do, without previously ascertaining the way and spirit of their penitent. And if they do not understand the matter, it is not for them to interfere in

what they do not comprehend, but rather to leave their penitent to others who understand him better than they. It is not a light fault to cause by a wrong direction the loss of inestimable blessings, and to endanger a soul. Thus, he who rashly errs, being under an obligation to give good advice – for so is everyone in the office he assumes – shall not go unpunished for the evil he has done. The affairs of God are to be handled with great caution and watchful circumspection, and especially this, which is so delicate, and so high, and where the gain is infinite if the direction given be right, and the loss also infinite if it be wrong.

61. But if you say that such a director may be excused – though for my part I do not see how – you must at least admit that he is inexcusable who keeps a penitent in his power for certain empty reasons and considerations known only to himself: he will not go unpunished. It is quite certain that a soul which is to make progress in the spiritual life, and which God is ever helping, must change its method of prayer, and be in need of a higher direction and of another spirit than those of such a director. Not all directors have the knowledge which every event on the spiritual road requires: neither are they all qualified to determine how a given soul is to be directed under every circumstance of the spiritual life; at least they must not presume that they are, or that it is God's will that a particular soul shall not advance further. As it is not everyone who can trim a block of wood, can also carve an image out of it; nor can everyone form the outlines who can carve; nor can everyone who fashions the outlines paint them, as neither can everyone who can paint perfect and complete the image: for every one of these can do only what he understands himself; and if any one of them were to attempt that which is not within the compass of his skill, he would spoil the statue.

62. So is it in the spiritual life; for if a director whose only work it is to trim the rude block, that is, to make his penitent despise the world, and mortify his desires; or if, further, it be that of the carver, who is to guide the soul into holy meditations, and his science extend no further, how can he guide his penitent to the highest perfection of the finished portrait, to that delicate colouring which consists not in the rough hewing of the wood, nor in the carving thereof, nor even in the formation of the outlines, but is rather a work which God himself perfects in the soul with his own hand? It is therefore quite certain that such a director as this, whose teaching is ever the same, cannot help driving back the penitent whom he subjects to it, or, at the least, hindering his advancement. For what will be the state of the image, if nothing be done to it but to rough-hew the wood and beat it with a mallet? What is this, but the discipline of the faculties? When shall the image be finished? When shall it be ready for God to colour it?

63. Is it possible that any spiritual director can think himself qualified for all this? That he looks upon himself as sufficiently skilful, so as to render the teaching of another needless for his penitent? Granting even that he is qualified for the whole direction of a particular soul, because, perhaps, such a soul has no vocation for a higher walk, it is almost impossible that he can be also a sufficient guide for all whom he hinders from passing out of his hands into the hands of others. God leads every soul by a separate path, and you will scarcely meet with one spirit which agrees with another in one half of the way by which it advances. Who can be like St Paul, who 'became all things to all men, that he might save all' (1 Cor. 9.22)?

64. Thou art thus become a tyrant of souls, the robber of their liberties, claiming for thyself all the freedom of the evangelical doctrine, and taking care that none of thy penitents leave thee; yea, still

further, and much worse, should it come to thy knowledge that any of them had gone elsewhere for direction, or to discuss a question which it was not convenient to submit to thee; or if God had led them for the purpose of learning what thou teachest not – I say it with shame – thou art jealous, like a husband of his wife. This is not zeal for the honour of God, but the zeal which cometh out of thine own pride and presumption. How couldest thou be sure that thy penitent had no need of other guidance than thine? With such directors God is angry and he threatens to chastise them, saying: 'Woe to the shepherds of Israel . . . you eat the milk and you clothed yourself with the wool . . . but my flock you did not feed . . . I will require my flock at their hand' (Ezek. 34.2, 10).

65. These directors, therefore, ought to leave their penitents at liberty, yea, they lie under an obligation to allow them to have recourse to the advice of others, and always to receive them again with a cheerful countenance; for they know not by what way God intends to lead them, especially when their present direction is not suited to them. That, indeed, is a sign that God is leading their penitents by another road, and that they require another director; they should, therefore, counsel the change, for a contrary course of proceeding springs from a foolish pride and presumption.

66. Let me now pass on from this and speak of other means, fatal as the plague, which these directors, or others worse than they, make use of in the guidance of souls. When God sends into a soul the unctions of holy desires, and leads it to give up the world, draws it on to change its state of life, and to serve him by despising the world – it is a great matter in his eyes that souls should have advanced to this, for the things of the world are not according to the heart of God – these directors, with their human reasonings and worldly motives, contrary to the doctrine of Christ, at variance

with mortification and contempt of all things, consulting their own interest or pleasure, or fearing where no fear is, interpose delays or suggest difficulties, or, what is worse, take away all such good thoughts from the hearts of their penitents. These directors have an evil spirit, are undevout and exceedingly worldly; unaccustomed to the ways of Christ, they do not enter in themselves by the narrow gate, neither will they suffer others to enter. These are they whom our Lord threatens in the gospel, saying: 'Woe to you lawyers, for you have taken away the key of knowledge: you yourselves have not entered in, and those that were entering you have hindered' (Luke 11.52).

67. These directors are in truth like barriers before the gate of heaven, forgetting that God has called them to the functions they exercise that they may compel those to enter in whom he has invited. He has given them this charge in the gospel, but they, on the contrary, compel their penitents not to enter in by the narrow gate which leadeth unto life (Matt. 7.13–14). Such a director as this is one of the blind guides who thwarts the direction of the Holy Ghost. This happens in many ways; some err knowingly; others ignorantly; but both the one and the other shall be punished; for by taking upon themselves the office which they fill, they are bound to understand and consider what they do.

68. The other blind guide that disturbs the soul in this interior recollection is Satan, who, being blind himself, desires to render the soul blind also. He labours, therefore, when the soul has entered into those deep solitudes wherein the delicate unctions of the Holy Ghost are infused – he hates and envies the soul for this, because he sees it fly beyond his reach, adorned with the riches of God – to throw over the soul's detachment and estrangement from the world, certain cataracts of knowledge, and the darkness of sensible sweetness,

sometimes good, the more to entice the soul, and to draw it back to the way of sense. He would have it fix its eyes on this, and make use of it with a view of drawing near to God, relying upon this kind of knowledge, and sensible sweetness. By this means Satan distracts the soul, and easily withdraws it from that solitude and recollection wherein the Holy Ghost worketh secretly his great marvels within.

69. And then the soul, naturally prone to sensible satisfaction and sweetness – especially if it aims at them – is most easily led to rely upon such knowledge and sweetness, and so draws back from the solitude wherein God was working. For as the soul, as it seemed, was doing nothing then, this new way appears preferable, because it is something, while solitude seemed to be nothing. How sad it is that the soul, not understanding its own state, should, for one mouthful, disqualify itself for feeding upon God himself; for he offers himself to be its food when he absorbs it in these spiritual and solitary unctions of his mouth.

70. In this way, the evil spirit, for a mere nothing, inflicts upon souls the very greatest injuries, causing the loss of great riches, and dragging them forth, like fish with a trifling bait, out of the depths of the pure waters of the spirit, where they were engulfed and drowned in God, resting upon no created support. He drags them to the bank, and supplies them with objects whereon to rest, and makes them walk on the earth painfully, that they may not float on 'the waters of Shiloah that run with silence' (Isa. 8.6), bathed in the unctions of God. It is wonderful how much Satan makes of this: and as a slight injury inflicted on the soul in this state is a great one, you will scarcely meet with one which has gone this way that has not suffered great injuries and incurred grievous losses. Satan stations himself with great cunning on the frontiers between sense and

spirit; there he deludes the soul, and feeds the senses, interposing sensible things to keep it back, and hinder it from escaping out of his hands.

71. The soul, too, is most easily taken by these devices, for it knows as yet of nothing better; neither does it dream that this is a loss; yea, rather, it looks on it as a great gain, and accepts the suggestions of the evil one gladly, for it thinks that God has come to visit it; consequently it omits to enter into the inner chamber of the Bridegroom, and stands at the door to see what is passing without in the sensual part of itself.

72. The devil, in the words of Job, 'seeth every high thing' that relates to souls that he may assail them (Job 41.34). If, therefore, a soul becomes recollected, he labours to disturb it by horrors and fears, or by bodily pains, or outward noise and tumults, that he may ruin it; he strives to draw its attention to the tumult he excites, and to fix it upon what is passing without, and to withdraw it from the interior spirit, but when he fails in his efforts he leaves it alone. So easily does Satan squander great riches and bring about the ruin of these precious souls, though he thinks this of more consequence than the fall of many others, that he looks upon it as a small matter because of the ease with which he effects it and because of the little trouble it costs him.

73. We may also understand in the same sense the following words spoken by God to Job: 'Lo! he shall absorb the river and shall not marvel: and he hath confidence that Jordan' – the highest perfection – 'may run into his mouth. In his eyes as with a hook he shall take him, and with stakes he shall bore through his nostrils' (Job 40.23–24). That is, he will turn away the soul from true spirituality by means of the arrows of distinct knowledge wherewith he pierces it, for the breath which goeth out through the nostrils in one volume becomes

dispersed if the nostrils be pierced, and escapes through the divers perforations.

74. Again it is said, 'The beams of the sun shall be under him, and he shall strew gold under as dirt' (Job 41.30). He causes souls that have been enlightened to lose the marvellous beams of divine knowledge, takes away and disperses abroad the precious gold of the divine adorning by which souls had been made rich.

75. O souls, now that God shows you mercies so great, leading you into solitude and recollection, withdrawing you from the labours of sense, do not return thereto. If your own exertions were once profitable, enabling you to deny the world and your own selves when you were but beginners, cease from them now when God of his mercy has begun to work in you, for now they will only embarrass you. If you will be careful to lay no stress on your own operations, withdrawing them from all things, and involving them in nothing – which is your duty in your present state – and wait lovingly and sincerely upon God at the same time – doing no violence to yourselves except to detach yourselves wholly, so as not to disturb your tranquillity and peace – God himself will feed you with the heavenly food, since you cease to hinder him.

76. The third blind guide of the soul is the soul itself, which, not understanding its own state, disturbs and injures itself. For as the soul knows of no operations except those of sense, when God leads it into solitude, where it cannot exert its faculties and elicit the acts it elicited before, and as it appears to itself then to be doing nothing, it strives to elicit its previous acts more distinctly and more sensibly. The consequence is distraction, dryness and disgust in that very soul which once delighted in the calm peace and spiritual silence, wherein God himself was in secret infusing his sweetness. It sometimes happens that God persists in keeping the soul in this quiet calm, and

that the soul persists in crying out with the imagination, and in walking with the understanding. Such souls are like children in their mothers' arms, who, unable to walk, cry, and struggle with their feet, demanding to be allowed to walk alone, but who cannot walk themselves, and suffer not their mothers to do so either. These souls make God resemble a painter whose work is hindered because the subject he portrays will not be still.

77. The soul, then, should keep in mind that it is now making greater progress than it could make by any efforts of its own, though it be wholly unconscious of that progress. God himself is carrying it in his own arms, and thus it happens that it is not aware that it is advancing. Though it thinks that it is doing nothing, yet in truth more is done than if itself were the agent; for God himself is working. If this work be invisible, that is nothing strange, for the work of God in the soul is not cognizable by sense, because silently wrought: 'The words of the wise are heard in silence' (Eccles. 9.17). Let the soul abandon itself to the hands of God and trust in him. He that will do so shall walk securely, for there is no danger then unless the soul should attempt anything in its own strength, or by the wilful exercise of its proper faculties.

78. Let us now return to the deep caverns of the senses, in which I said the sufferings of the soul are ordinarily very great when God is anointing it, and preparing it for union with himself by his subtle and delicate unctions. These unctions of God are so subtle that, penetrating into the inmost depths of the soul, they so dispose it, and so fill it with sweetness, that the sufferings and fainting of the soul through its great desire in the immense void of the caverns are immeasurable. Now if the unction which disposes the caverns for the union of the spiritual marriage be so wonderful, what shall the accomplishment thereof be? Certain it is that as the hunger and thirst

and suffering of the caverns, so will be the satisfaction, fullness, and delight thereof. According to the perfection of these dispositions will be the delight of the fruition and possession of the sense of the soul, which is the power and energy of its very substance for perceiving and delighting in the objects of its faculties.

79. These faculties are with great propriety called caverns. For as the soul is conscious that they admit the profound intelligence and splendours of the lamps, it sees clearly also that they are deep in proportion to the depth of the intelligence and love; that they have space and capacity commensurate with the distinct sources of the intelligence, of the sweetness and delight which it receives in them. All this is received and established in the cavern of the sense of the soul which is the capacity thereof for possession, perception and fruition. Thus, as the common sense of the imagination is the place where all the objects of the outward senses are treasured up, so is this common sense of the soul enlightened and made rich by a possession so grand and so glorious.

'Dim and dark'

80. The eye sees not for two reasons; either because it is in darkness or is blind. God is the light and the true object of the soul, and when he does not shine upon it, it is then in darkness, though its power of vision may be most perfect. When the soul is in sin, or when it occupies the desires with other things than God, it is then blind. Though the light of God be not wanted to it then, yet, being blind, it cannot see the light because of its blindness, which is the practical ignorance in which it lives. Before God enlightened the soul in its transformation it was in darkness and ignorant of his great goodness, as was the wise man before he was enlightened, for he says, 'He enlightened my ignorance.'[17]

81. Speaking spiritually, it is one thing to be blind and another to be in darkness. Blindness proceeds from sin, but darkness does not necessarily involve sin, and it happens in two ways. There is natural darkness where the light of natural things shines not, and there is supernatural darkness where there is no knowledge of many supernatural things. Here the soul says with regard to them both, that the understanding without God abided in darkness. For until our Lord said, 'Let light be' (Gen. 1.3), darkness was upon the face of the deep of the cavern of the soul's sense. The deeper the cavern when God shines not upon it, the deeper is the darkness thereof. Thus it is impossible for it to lift up the eyes to the divine light; yea the divine light is not even thought of, because never seen or known to exist; there is therefore no desire for it. And the soul desires darkness rather than light, and so goes on from darkness to darkness, led by darkness, for darkness can lead only to darkness again.

82. David saith, 'day to day uttereth word and night to night showeth knowledge' (Ps. 19.2), thus as the deep of darkness calleth another deep, and the deep of light another deep of light (Ps. 42.7); like calling upon like, so the light of grace which God had before given to the soul, and by which he opened the eyes of it from the deep to behold the divine light, and made it pleasing to himself, calls to another deep of grace, namely, the divine transformation of the soul in God, wherein the eye of sense is enlightened and rendered pleasing.

83. The eye was also blind in that it took pleasure in other than God. The blindness of the higher and rational sense is caused by the desire which, like a cloud or a cataract, overlies and covers the eye of reason, so that it shall not see what is before it. Thus, then, the grandeur and magnificence of the divine beauty are rendered invisible, so far as the pleasure of sense is followed. For if we cover

the eye with anything, however trifling it may be, that is enough to obstruct the vision of objects before us be they ever so large. Thus, then, a single desire entertained by the soul suffices to hinder the vision of all the divine grandeurs which are higher than its desires and longings. Who can say how impossible it is for the soul, subject to desires, to judge of the things of God? For he that would judge aright of these must cast away all desires, because he cannot judge aright while subject thereto; for in that case he will come to consider the things of God not to be God's, and those things which are not God's to be the things of God.

84. While this cloud and cataract cover the eye of the judgement, nothing is visible except the cloud, sometimes of one colour, sometimes of another, according to circumstances, and men will take the cloud for God, because they see nothing beside the cloud which overshadows the sense, and God is not comprehended by sense. Thus, desire and sensual satisfactions hinder the knowledge of high things, as it is written, 'The bewitching of vanity obscureth good things, and the inconstancy of concupiscence perverteth the understanding' that is without malice (Wisd. 4.12). Those persons, therefore, who are not so spiritual as to be purified from their desires and inclinations, but are still sensual, believe those things to be important which are in truth of no account in spirituality, being intimately connected with sense; they take no account of and despise the deep things of the spirit, which are further removed from sense; yea sometimes they look upon them as folly, as we learn from St Paul, 'The sensual man perceiveth not these things that are of the Spirit of God: for it is foolishness to him and he cannot understand' (1 Cor. 2.14).

85. The sensual man is he who still lives according to the desires and inclinations of nature, and even though these desires come occasionally into contact with the things of the spirit, yet, if a man cleaves

to spiritual things with his natural desires, they are still natural desires only. The spirituality of the object is little to the purpose, if the desire of it proceed from itself, having its root and strength in nature. What! you will say, is it not a supernatural desire to desire God? No, not always; but only then when the motive is supernatural, and when the strength of the desire proceeds from God; that is a very different thing. When the desire comes from thyself, so far as it relates to the manner thereof, it is nothing more than natural. So, then, when thou art attached to thy spiritual tastes, exerting thine own natural desire, thou bringest a cataract over thine eye, thou art sensual, incapable of perceiving or judging what is spiritual, for that transcends all natural sense and desire.

86. If thou still doubtest, I have nothing further to add except to bid thee read over again what I have written, and that done perhaps the doubts will vanish. What I have said is the substance of the truth, and I cannot now enlarge upon it. The sense of the soul hitherto in darkness, without the divine light and blinded by its desires, is now such that its deep caverns, because of the divine union, 'with unwonted brightness give light and warmth together to the Beloved'.

'With unwonted brightness
Give light and warmth together to the Beloved'

87. These caverns of the soul's faculties being now in a wonderful way among the marvellous splendours of the lamps which burn within them, being lighted and burning in God, remit back to God in God, in addition to their self-surrender to him, those very splendours which they receive from him in loving bliss; they also, turning to God in God, being themselves lamps burning in the brightness of the divine lamps, return to the Beloved that very light and warmth of love which they receive from him. Now, indeed, they give back

unto him, in the way they receive them, those very splendours which he communicates, as crystal reflects the rays of the sun; but in a nobler manner, because of the intervention of the will.

'With unwonted brightness'

88. That is, strange and surpassing all imagination and description. For the perfection of beauty wherein the soul restores to God what it has received from him is now in conformity with that perfection wherewith the understanding – made one with that of God – received the divine wisdom: and the perfection wherewith the will restores to God in God that very goodness he gave it – for it was given only to be restored – is in conformity with that perfection wherein the will is united with the will of God. In the same way, proportional to the perfection of its knowledge of God's greatness, united therewith, does the soul shine and give forth the warmth of love. And according to the perfection of the other divine attributes communicated to the soul, such as strength, beauty, justice, are those perfections wherewith the spiritual mind, now in enjoyment, gives back to the Beloved in the Beloved the very light and warmth which it is receiving from him.

89. The soul now being one with God is itself God by participation, and though not so perfectly as it will be in the world to come, is still, as I have said, as God in a shadow.[18] Thus, then, the soul, by reason of transformation, being a shadow of God, effects through God in God what he effects within it himself by himself, because the will of both is one. And as God is giving himself with a free and gracious will, so the soul also with a will, the more free and the more generous the more it is united with God in God, is, as it were, giving back to God – in that loving complacency with which it regards the divine essence and perfections – God himself.

90. This is a mystic and affective gift of the soul to God, for then the soul seems in truth to have God for its own possession, and that it possesses him, as his adopted child, by right of ownership, by the free gift of himself made unto it. The soul gives to the Beloved, who is God himself, what he had given to it. Herein it pays the whole debt, for the soul giveth as much voluntarily with inestimable joy and delight, giving the Holy Spirit as its own of its own free will, so that God may be loved as he deserves to be.

91. Herein consists the inestimable joy of the soul, for it sees that it offers to God what becomes him in his infinite being. Though it be true that the soul cannot give God to God anew, because he is always himself in himself, still it does so, perfectly and wisely, giving all that he has given it in requital of his love; this is to give as it is given, and God is repaid by this gift of the soul; nothing less could repay him. He receives this gift of the soul as if it were its own, with kindness and grace, in the sense I have explained; and in that gift he loves it anew, and gives himself freely to it, and the soul also loves him anew. Thus, there is in fact a mutual interchange of love between the soul and God in the conformity of the union, and in the matrimonial surrender, wherein the goods of both, that is, the divine essence, are possessed by both together, in the voluntary giving up of each to the other. God and the soul say, the one to the other, what the Son of God said to the Father, 'All my things are thine, and thine are mine, and I am glorified in them' (John 17.10). This will be verified in the fruition of the next life without intermission, and is verified in the state of union when the soul's communion with God energizes in an act of love.

92. The soul can offer such a gift, though far greater than itself, just as he who possesses many kingdoms and nations as his own, though greater than he, can bestow them upon whom he will. This

is the soul's great delight that it sees itself giving unto God more than itself is worth, that it gives himself to God so generously, as if God were its own, in that divine light and warmth of love which he himself has given it. This is effected in the life to come through the light of glory and of love, and in this life by faith most enlightened and by love most enkindled. Thus it is that the deep caverns of sense, with unwonted brightness give light and heat together to the Beloved. I say together, because the communication of the Father and of the Son and of the Holy Ghost in the soul is one; they are the light and the fire of love therein.

93. I must here observe briefly on the perfection of beauty where-with the soul makes this gift. In the act of union, as the soul enjoys a certain image of fruition, caused by the union of the understand-ing and will in God, it makes this gift of God to God, and of itself to him, in most wonderful ways; delighting itself therein, and con-strained thereto. As to love, the soul stands before God in strange beauty, as to the shadow of fruition in the same way, and also as to praise and gratitude.

94. As to the first, which is love, the soul has three grand perfec-tions of beauty. It loves God by means of God. This is an admirable perfection, because, set on fire by the Holy Ghost, and having the Holy Ghost dwelling within it, it loves as the Father loves the Son, as it is written, 'that the love wherewith thou hast loved me, may be in them, and I in them' (John 17.26). The second perfection is that it loves God in God, for in this union the soul is vehemently absorbed in the love of God, and God communicates himself with great vehemence to it. The third perfection of beauty is that the soul now loves God for what he is; for it loves him not merely because he is bountiful, good and generous to it, but much more earnestly, because he is all this essentially in himself.

95. There are also three perfections of beauty in that shadow of fruition, marvellously great. The first is that the soul enjoys God here, united with God himself, for as the understanding of the soul is one with wisdom and goodness, and perceives so clearly – though not perfectly as in the life to come – it delights greatly in all these, clearly understood, as I said before.[19] The second perfection of beauty is that the soul delights itself in God alone without the admixture of any created thing. The third is that it enjoys him alone as he is, without the admixture of any selfish feeling, or of any created object.

96. There are also three principal perfections of beauty in the praise of God which the soul offers to him in union. The first is that the soul offers it as an act of duty, because it recognizes this as the end of its creation; as it is written, 'This people have I formed for myself, they shall show forth my praise' (Isa. 43.21). The second is that it praises him for blessings received, and because of the joy it has in praising our Lord who is so great. The third is that it praises him for what he is in himself, for if the praises of God were unaccompanied by any pleasure at all, still it would praise him because he is who he is.

97. Gratitude also has three principal perfections. The first is thanksgiving for all natural and spiritual blessings, and for all benefits received. The second is the great delight of praising God, in the way of thanksgiving, for the soul is moved with great vehemence in the act. The third is that the soul gives thanks unto God only because he is, which is much more efficacious and more delightful.

Stanza 4

How gently and how lovingly
Thou awakest in my bosom,
Where thou secretly dwellest alone;
And in thy sweet breathing,
Full of grace and glory,
How tenderly thou fillest me with thy love.

Explanation

Here the soul turns towards the Bridegroom in great love, magnifying him and giving him thanks for two marvellous graces which he sometimes effects within the soul through its union with himself. The soul, too, observes on the way he produces them and on their effects upon itself.

2. The first effect is the awakening of God in the soul, and that in gentleness and love. The second is the breathing of God in the soul, and that in grace and bliss given in that breathing. The effect of this upon the soul is to make it love him sweetly and tenderly. The stanza therefore may be paraphrased as follows: O how gently and how lovingly dost thou lie awake in the depth and centre of my soul, where thou in secret and in silence alone, as its sole Lord, abidest, not only as in thine own house or in thine own chamber, but also as within my own bosom, in close and intimate union: O how gently and how lovingly! Sweet to me is thy breathing in that

awakening, for it is full of grace and glory. O with what tenderness dost thou inspire me with love of thee! The figure is borrowed from one awaking from sleep, and drawing his breath, for the soul in this state feels it to be so.

'How gently and how lovingly
Thou awakest in my bosom'

3. The awakenings of God in the soul are manifold, and so many that were I to describe them I should never end. This awakening, to which the soul refers here, the work of the Son of God, is, in my opinion, of the highest kind, and the source of the greatest good to the soul. This awakening is a movement of the Word in the depth of the soul of such grandeur, authority and glory, and of such profound sweetness, that all the balsams, all the aromatic herbs and flowers of the world seem to be mingled and shaken together for the production of that sweetness: that all the kingdoms and dominions of the world, all the powers and virtues of heaven are moved; this is not the whole, all the virtues, substance, perfections and graces of all created things shine forth and make the same movement in unison together. For as St John saith, 'What was made in him was life',[20] and in him moves and lives; as the Apostle says, 'In him we live and move and are' (Acts 17.28).

4. The reason is this: when the grand Emperor would reveal himself to the soul, moving himself in the light he gives, and yet not moving in it – he, upon whose shoulder is the principality (Isa. 9.6), that is, the three worlds of heaven, earth and hell, and all that is in them, and who sustains all by the word of his power (Heb. 1.3) – then all seem to move together. As when the earth moves, all natural things upon it move with it; so is it when the Prince moves, for he carries his court, not the court him. This,

however, is an exceedingly imperfect illustration; for here not only all seem to move, but also to manifest their being, their beauty, power and loveliness, the root of their duration and life in him. There, indeed, the soul sees how all creatures, higher and lower, live, continue and energize in him, and understands the words of the wise man, 'by me kings reign . . . by me princes rule, and the mighty decree justice' (Prov. 8.15).

5. Though it is true that the soul here sees that all these things are distinct from God, in that they have a created existence, it understands them in him with their force, origin and strength; it knows also that God in his own essence is, in an infinitely pre-eminent way, all these things, so that it understands them better in him, their first cause, than in themselves. This is the great joy of this awakening, namely, to know creatures in God, and not God in his creatures: this is to know effects in their cause, and not cause by its effects.

6. This movement in the soul is wonderful, for God himself moves not. Without movement on the part of God, the soul is renewed and moved by him; the divine life and being and the harmony of creation are revealed with marvellous newness, the cause assuming the designation of the effect resulting from it. If we regard the effect, we may say with the wise man that God moves, 'for wisdom is more moveable than all moveable things', not because it moves itself but because it is the source and principle of all motion, and 'permanently in herself, she reneweth all things'; this is the meaning of the words, 'more moveable than all moveable things' (Wisd. 7.24).

7. Thus, then, strictly speaking, in this movement it is the soul that is moved and awakened, and the expression 'awake' is correct. God, however, being always, as the soul sees him, the mover, the ruler and

the giver of life, power, graces and gifts to all creatures, contains all in himself; virtually, actually and supremely. The soul beholds what God is in himself, and what he is in creatures. So may we see, when the palace is thrown open, in one glance, both the magnificence of him who inhabits it and what he is doing. This, according to my understanding of it, is this awakening and vision of the soul; it is as if God drew back some of the many veils and coverings that are before it, so that it might see what he is; then indeed – but still dimly, because all the veils are not drawn back, that of faith remaining – the divine face full of grace bursts through and shines, which, as it moves all things by its power, appears together with the effect it produces, and this is the awakening of the soul.

8. Though all that is good in man comes from God, and though man of himself can do nothing that is good, it may be said in truth, that our awakening is the awakening of God, and our rising the rising of God. 'Arise, why sleepest thou, O Lord?' saith the Psalmist (Ps. 44.23). That is in effect to say, 'Raise us up and awake us, for we are fallen and asleep.' Thus then, because the soul had fallen asleep, and could never rouse itself again, and because it is God alone who can open its eyes, and effect its awakening, this awakening is most properly referred to God: 'Thou awakest in my bosom.'

'Thou awakest in my bosom'

9. Awake us, O Lord, and enlighten us, that we may know and love the good things which thou hast set always before us, and we shall know that thou art moved to do us good, and hast had us in remembrance. It is utterly impossible to describe what the soul, in this awakening, knows and feels of the majesty of God, in the inmost depths of its being, that is, its bosom. For in the soul resounds an infinite power, with the voice of a multitude of perfections, of

thousands and thousands of virtues, wherein itself abiding and sub-sisting, becomes 'terrible as an army set in array' (Song of Songs 6.3), sweet and gracious in him who comprehends in himself all the sweetness, and all the graces of his creation.

10. But here comes the question: how can the soul bear so vehe-ment a communication while in the flesh, when in truth it has not strength for it without fainting away? The mere sight of Ahasuerus on his throne, in his royal robe, glittering with gold and precious stones, was so terrible in the eyes of Esther, that she fainted through fear, so awful was his face. 'I saw thee, my lord, as an angel of God, and my heart was troubled, for fear of thy glory' (Esth. 15.13–14). Glory oppresses him who beholds it, if it does not glorify him. How much more then is the soul now liable to faint away, when it beholds not an angel but God himself, the Lord of the angels, with his face full of the beauty of all creatures, of terrible power and glory, and the voice of the multitude of his perfections. It is to this that Job referred when he said, 'We have heard scarce a little drop of his word; who shall be able to behold the thunder of his greatness?' (Job 26.14), and again, 'I will not that he contend with me with much strength, nor that he oppress me with the weight of his greatness' (Job 23.6).

11. The soul, however, does not faint away and tremble at this awakening so powerful and glorious. There are two reasons for this: one is that it is now in the state of perfection, and therefore the lower portion of it is purified and conformed to the spirit, exempt from that pain and loss which spiritual communications involve, when the sense and spirit are not purified and disposed for the reception of them. The second and the principal reason is that referred to in the first line of this stanza, namely, that God shows himself gentle and loving. For as he shows his greatness and glory to the soul in

order to comfort and exalt it, so does he favour and strengthen it also, and sustain its natural powers while manifesting his greatness gently and lovingly. This is easy enough to him, who with his right hand protected Moses that he might behold his glory (Exod. 33.22).

12. Thus the soul feels God's love and gentleness to be commensurate with his power, authority and greatness, for in him these are all one. Its delight is therefore vehement, and the protection it receives strong in gentleness and love, so that itself being made strong may be able without fainting away to sustain this vehement joy. Esther, indeed, fainted away, but that was because the king seemed unfavourable towards her, for with 'burning eyes' he 'showed the wrath of his breast' (Esth. 15.7). But the moment he looked graciously upon her, touched her with his sceptre and kissed her, she recovered herself, for he had said to her, 'I am thy brother, fear not.'

13. So is it with the soul in the presence of the King of kings, for the moment he shows himself as its Bridegroom and Brother, all fear vanishes away. Because in showing unto it, in gentleness and not in anger, the strength of his power and the love of his goodness, he communicates to it the strength and love of his breast, 'leaping from his throne' (Esth. 15.8) to caress it, as the bridegroom from his secret chamber, touching it with the sceptre of his majesty, and as a brother embracing it. There the royal robes and the fragrance thereof, which are the marvellous attributes of God; there the splendour of gold which is charity, and the glittering of the precious stones of supernatural knowledge; and there the face of the Word full of grace, strike the queenly soul, so that, transformed in the virtues of the King of Heaven, it beholds itself, a queen: with the Psalmist, therefore, may it be said of it, and with truth, 'The queen stood on thy right hand in gilded clothing, surrounded with variety' (Ps. 45.9). And as all this

passes in the very depths of the soul, it is added immediately, 'Where thou secretly dwellest alone'.

'Where thou secretly dwellest alone'

14. He is said to dwell secretly in the soul's bosom, because, as I have said,[21] this sweet embracing takes place in the inmost substance and powers of the soul. We must keep in mind that God dwells in a secret and hidden way in all souls, in their very substance, for if he did not, they could not exist at all. This dwelling of God is very different in different souls; in some he dwells alone, in others not; in some he dwells contented, in others displeased; in some as in his own house, giving his orders, and ruling it; in others, as a stranger in a house not his own, where he is not permitted to command, or to do anything at all. Where personal desires and self-will least abound, there is he most alone, most contented, there he dwells as in his own house, ruling and directing it, and the more secretly he dwells, the more he is alone.

15. So then in that soul wherein no desire dwells, and out of which all images and forms of created things have been cast, the Beloved dwells most secretly himself, and the purer the soul and the greater its estrangement from everything but God, the more intimate his converse and the closer his embrace. He dwells there then in secret, for Satan cannot come near his dwelling place, nor see the embracing; nor can any understanding explain it. But he is not hidden from the soul in the state of perfection, for such a soul is ever conscious of his presence. Only in these awakenings he seems to awake who before was asleep in the soul's bosom; and though it felt and enjoyed his presence, he seemed as one sleeping within.

16. O how blessed is that soul which is ever conscious of God reposing and resting within it. How necessary it is for such a soul to flee from the matters of this world, to live in great tranquillity, so that nothing whatever shall disturb the Beloved 'at his repose'.

17. He is there as it were asleep in the embraces of the soul, and the soul is, in general, conscious of his presence, and, in general, delights exceedingly in it. If he were always awake in the soul, the communications of knowledge and love would be unceasing, and that would be a state of glory. If he awakes but once, merely opening his eyes, and affects the soul so profoundly, what would become of it if he were continually awake within it?

18. He dwells secretly in other souls, those which have not attained to this state of union, not indeed displeased, though they are not yet perfectly disposed for union: these souls in general are not conscious of his presence, but only during the time of these sweet awakenings, which however are not of the same kind with those already described, neither indeed are they to be compared with them. But the state of these souls is not so secret from the devil, nor so far above the reach of the understanding as the other, because the senses always furnish some indications of it by the excitement into which they are thrown. The senses are not perfectly annihilated before the union is complete, and they manifest their power in some degree, because they are not yet wholly spiritual. But in this awakening of the Bridegroom in the perfect soul, all is perfect because he effects it all himself in the way I have spoken of. In this awakening, as of one aroused from sleep and drawing breath, the soul feels the breathing of God, and therefore it says: 'In thy sweet breathing'.

'And in thy sweet breathing,
Full of grace and glory,
How tenderly thou fillest me with thy love'

19. I would not speak of this breathing of God, neither do I wish to do so, because I am certain that I cannot; and indeed were I to speak of it, it would seem then to be something less than what it is in reality. This breathing of God is in the soul, in which in the awakening of the deep knowledge of the Divinity, he breathes the Holy Ghost according to the measure of that knowledge which absorbs it most profoundly, which inspires it most tenderly with love according to what it saw. This breathing is full of grace and glory, and therefore the Holy Ghost fills the soul with goodness and glory, whereby he inspires it with the love of himself, transcending all glory and all understanding. This is the reason why I say nothing more.

Notes

1 See *Spiritual Canticle*, Stanzas 26.4, 14; 38.2; 39.20.

2 These stanzas were written after the saint's escape from the prison of the friars in Toledo, and the commentary on them was written at the request of Doña Ana de Peñalosa, one of his penitents.

3 *Dark Night*, Book 2. The former editions, and all the translations, say 'in the treatise of the *Dark Night* and in that of the *Ascent of Mount Carmel*', as if the saint had spoken on this subject in both works. The manuscripts make the matter clear, for St John considered the *Dark Night* as part of the *Ascent*.

4 St Gregory, *Homilia 30* in *Evangelium* (Whit Sunday): 'Intus facta sunt corda flammantia, quia dum Deum in ignis visione susceperunt, per amorem suaviter arserunt.'

5 *Roman Breviary*, Thursday within the Octave of Pentecost, First Response at Matins: 'Advenit ignis divinus, non comburens, sed illuminans.'

6 See *St Teresa: The Book of Her Life*, 29.17 (transverberation of her heart).

7 Stanza 1.7.

8 Stanza 1.10 (line 2).

9 *Spiritual Canticle*, 7.3.

10 'Qui ergo mente integra Deum desiderat, profecto jam habet quem amat', Hom. 30 in *Evangel.*

11 St Teresa, *Interior Castle*, 5 Mansion, 4.1, 2; 7 Mansion, 2.2.

12 St Teresa, *Life*, ch. 13, *passim*; *Way of Perfection*, 5.1, 2.

13 *Ascent of Mount Carmel*, Book 2, chs 13 and 15.1.

14 *Dark Night*, Book 1, ch. 8.

15 *Dark Night*, Book 1, ch. 9.

16 St Teresa, *Life*, ch. 18.18.

17 Ecclus. 2.26: 'Ignorantias meas illuminavit.' This text is no longer in the Vulgate. See *Dark Night*, Book 2, ch. 12.2.

18 See *Spiritual Canticle*, 34.6, 7.

19 See Stanza 3.17–19 above.

20 John 1.3. The Carmelite Breviary used by St John of the Cross until 1586 maintains the old punctuation: 'Without him was made nothing. What was made in him was life.'

21 Stanzas 1.9 and 2.9.

Flo's Story

A little story about prayer

After I was widowed, my daughter Jo persuaded me to go to this tea dance in a church hall, a bus ride away from where I live. It was a way to keep fit and meet a few people and really cheered me up, but I still felt empty inside.

One day Dot, the lady who runs the dances, was handing out these little *Prayers on the Move* booklets, so I took one. I hadn't been to church for years and I hadn't prayed for a long time, but reading this little book, by myself, in my own time, the prayers really spoke to me. I realized what had been missing.

The next week, I told Dot that I'd really enjoyed the book and said I thought it would be nice to go to church. Dot said she'd give me a lift. Now I'm going to church every Sunday, I've found my faith again and I'm so happy. That empty feeling inside has gone away and it's all thanks to a little booklet called *Prayers on the Move*.

Inspired by a true story. Names and places have been changed.

Help us to tell more stories like Flo's. Sign up for the newsletter, buy bags, books and travelcard wallets, and make a donation to help more people like Flo find God through a book. www.prayersonthemove.com.